studysync®

Reading & Writing Companion

Empathy

⠿studysync®

studysync.com

Send all inquiries to:
BookheadEd Learning, LLC
610 Daniel Young Drive
Sonoma, CA 95476

5 6 7 8 9 LWI 21 20 19 18 B

GETTING STARTED

Welcome to the StudySync Reading and Writing Companion! In this booklet, you will find a collection of readings based on the theme of the unit you are studying. As you work through the readings, you will be asked to answer questions and perform a variety of tasks designed to help you closely analyze and understand each text selection. Read on for an explanation of

CORE ELA TEXTS

In each Core ELA Unit you will read texts and text excerpts that share a common theme, despite their different genres, time periods, and authors. Each reading encourages a closer look with questions and a short writing assignment.

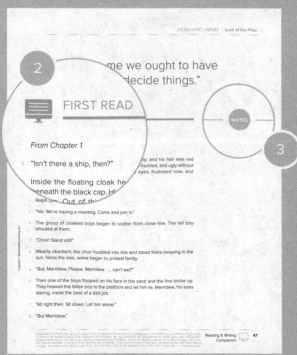

 INTRODUCTION

An Introduction to each text provides historical context for your reading as well as information about the author. You will also learn about the genre of the excerpt and the year in which it was written.

 FIRST READ

During your first reading of each excerpt, you should just try to get a general idea of the content and message of the reading. Don't worry if there are parts you don't understand or words that are unfamiliar to you. You'll have an opportunity later to dive deeper into the text.

 NOTES

Many times, while working through the activities after each text, you will be asked to **annotate** or **make annotations** about what you are reading. This means that you should highlight or underline words in the text and use the "Notes" column to make comments or jot down any questions you may have. You may also want to note any unfamiliar vocabulary words here.

4   THINK QUESTIONS

These questions will ask you to start thinking critically about the text, asking specific questions about its purpose, and making connections to your prior knowledge and reading experiences. To answer these questions, you should go back to the text and draw upon specific evidence that you find there to support your responses. You will also begin to explore some of the more challenging vocabulary words used in the excerpt.

5   CLOSE READ & FOCUS QUESTIONS

After you have completed the First Read, you will then be asked to go back and read the excerpt more closely and critically. Before you begin your Close Read, you should read through the Focus Questions to get an idea of the concepts you will want to focus on during your second reading. You should work through the Focus Questions by making annotations, highlighting important concepts, and writing notes or questions in the "Notes" column. Depending on instructions from your teacher, you may need to respond online or use a separate piece of paper to start expanding on your thoughts and ideas.

6   WRITING PROMPT

Your study of each excerpt or selection will end with a writing assignment. To complete this assignment, you should use your notes, annotations, and answers to both the Think and Focus Questions. Be sure to read the prompt carefully and address each part of it in your writing assignment.

ENGLISH LANGUAGE DEVELOPMENT TEXTS

The English Language Development texts and activities take a closer look at the language choices that authors make to communicate their ideas. Individual and group activities will help develop your understanding of each text.

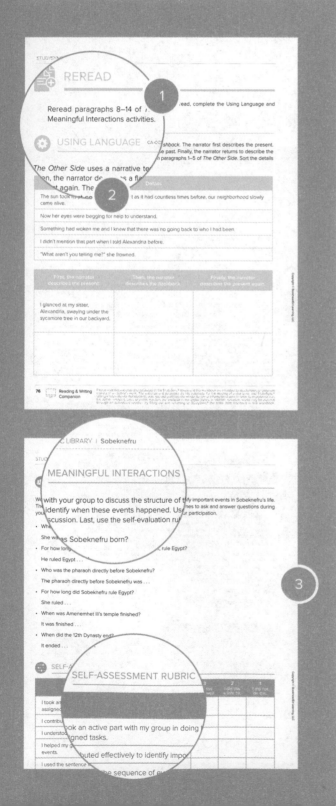

1 REREAD

After you have completed the First Read, you will have two additional opportunities to revisit portions of the excerpt more closely. The directions for each reread will specify which paragraphs or sections you should focus on.

2 USING LANGUAGE

These questions will ask you to analyze the author's use of language and conventions in the text. You may be asked to write in sentence frames, fill in a chart, or you may simply choose between multiple-choice options. To answer these questions, you should read the exercise carefully and go back in the text as necessary to accurately complete the activity.

3 MEANINGFUL INTERACTIONS & SELF-ASSESSMENT RUBRIC

After each reading, you will participate in a group activity or discussion with your peers. You may be provided speaking frames to guide your discussions or writing frames to support your group work. To complete these activities, you should revisit the excerpt for textual evidence and support. When you finish, use the Self-Assessment Rubric to evaluate how well you participated and collaborated.

EXTENDED WRITING PROJECT

The Extended Writing Project is your opportunity to explore the theme of each unit in a longer written work. You will draw information from your readings, research, and own life experiences to complete the assignment.

1 WRITING PROJECT

After you have read all of the unit text selections, you will move on to a writing project. Each project will guide you through the process of writing an argumentative, narrative, informative, or literary analysis essay. Student models and graphic organizers will provide guidance and help you organize your thoughts as you plan and write your essay. Throughout the project, you will also study and work on specific writing skills to help you develop different portions of your writing.

2 WRITING PROCESS STEPS

There are five steps in the writing process: **Prewrite, Plan, Draft, Revise,** and **Edit, Proofread, and Publish.** During each step, you will form and shape your writing project so that you can effectively express your ideas. Lessons focus on one step at a time, and you will have the chance to receive feedback from your peers and teacher.

3 WRITING SKILLS

Each Writing Skill lesson focuses on a specific strategy or technique that you will use during your writing project. The lessons begin by analyzing a student model or mentor text, and give you a chance to learn and practice the skill on its own. Then, you will have the opportunity to apply each new skill to improve the writing in your own project.

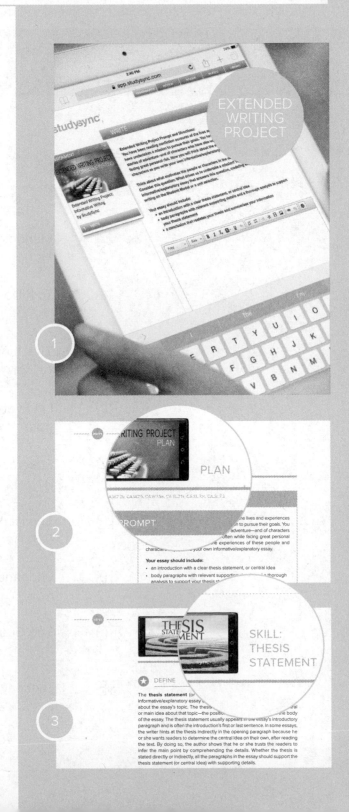

Empathy

 TEXTS

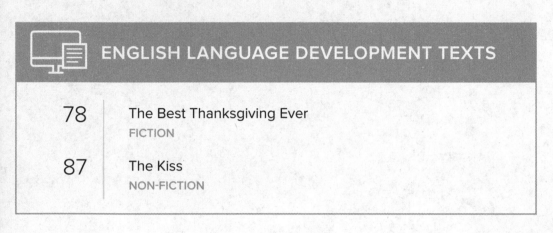

ENGLISH LANGUAGE DEVELOPMENT TEXTS

EXTENDED WRITING PROJECT

137

Text Fulfillment through StudySync

MARIGOLDS

FICTION

Eugenia Collier
1969

INTRODUCTION

In Eugenia Collier's powerful short story, "Marigolds," Lizabeth, the narrator, tells a story from her childhood in a dusty Depression-era town. Confused and amused by why the town outcast, Miss Lottie, puts so much care into the brilliantly colored patch of marigolds outside her crumbling gray shack, Lizabeth and her friends tease the old woman and throw rocks at her flowers. A later incident in the garden causes Lizabeth great shame, but leads to a deeper moral understanding, and a major change in her life.

"Miss Lottie's marigolds were perhaps the strangest part of the picture."

 FIRST READ

 NOTES

1   When I think of the hometown of my youth, all that I seem to remember is dust—the brown, crumbly dust of late summer—arid, sterile dust that gets into the eyes and makes them water, gets into the throat and between the toes of bare brown feet. I don't know why I should remember only the dust. Surely there must have been lush green lawns and paved streets under leafy shade trees somewhere in town; but memory is an abstract painting—it does not present things as they are, but rather as they *feel*. And so, when I think of that time and that place, I remember only the dry September of the dirt roads and grassless yards of the shantytown where I lived. And one other thing I remember, another incongruency of memory—a brilliant splash of sunny yellow against the dust—Miss Lottie's marigolds.

2   Whenever the memory of those marigolds flashes across my mind, a strange nostalgia comes with it and remains long after the picture has faded. I feel again the chaotic emotions of adolescence, illusive as smoke, yet as real as the potted geranium before me now. Joy and rage and wild animal gladness and shame become tangled together in the multicolored skein of fourteen-going-on-fifteen as I recall that devastating moment when I was suddenly more woman than child, years ago in Miss Lottie's yard. I think of those marigolds at the strangest times; I remember them vividly now as I desperately pass away the time.

3   I suppose that futile waiting was the sorrowful background music of our impoverished little community when I was young. The Depression that gripped the nation was no new thing to us, for the black workers of rural Maryland had always been depressed. I don't know what it was that we were waiting for; certainly not for the **prosperity** that was "just around the corner," for those were white folks' words, which we never believed. Nor did we wait for hard work and thrift to pay off in shining success, as the American Dream promised, for we knew better than that, too. Perhaps we waited for a miracle,

amorphous in concept but necessary if one were to have the grit to rise before dawn each day and labor in the white man's vineyard until after dark, or to wander about in the September dust offering one's sweat in return for some meager share of bread. But God was chary with miracles in those days, and so we waited—and waited.

4   We children, of course, were only vaguely aware of the extent of our poverty. Having no radios, few newspapers, and no magazines, we were somewhat unaware of the world outside our community. Nowadays we would be called culturally deprived and people would write books and hold conferences about us. In those days everybody we knew was just as hungry and ill clad as we were. Poverty was the cage in which we all were trapped, and our hatred of it was still the vague, undirected restlessness of the zoo-bred flamingo who knows that nature created him to fly free.

5   As I think of those days I feel most poignantly the tag end of summer, the bright, dry times when we began to have a sense of shortening days and the imminence of the cold.

6   By the time I was fourteen, my brother Joey and I were the only children left at our house, the older ones having left home for early marriage or the lure of the city, and the two babies having been sent to relatives who might care for them better than we. Joey was three years younger than I, and a boy, and therefore vastly inferior. Each morning our mother and father trudged wearily down the dirt road and around the bend, she to her domestic job, he to his daily unsuccessful quest for work. After our few chores around the tumbledown shanty, Joey and I were free to run wild in the sun with other children similarly situated.

7   For the most part, those days are ill-defined in my memory, running together and combining like a fresh watercolor painting left out in the rain. I remember squatting in the road drawing a picture in the dust, a picture which Joey gleefully erased with one sweep of his dirty foot. I remember fishing for minnows in a muddy creek and watching sadly as they eluded my cupped hands, while Joey laughed uproariously. And I remember, that year, a strange restlessness of body and of spirit, a feeling that something old and familiar was ending, and something unknown and therefore terrifying was beginning.

8   One day returns to me with special clarity for some reason, perhaps because it was the beginning of the experience that in some inexplicable way marked the end of innocence. I was loafing under the great oak tree in our yard, deep in some reverie which I have now forgotten, except that it involved some secret, secret thoughts of one of the Harris boys across the yard. Joey and a bunch of kids were bored now with the old tire suspended from an oak limb, which had kept them entertained for a while.

NOTES

9 "Hey, Lizabeth," Joey yelled. He never talked when he could yell. "Hey, Lizabeth, let's go somewhere."

10 I came reluctantly from my private world. "Where you want to go? What you want to do?"

11 The truth was that we were becoming tired of the formlessness of our summer days. The idleness whose prospect had seemed so beautiful during the busy days of spring now had **degenerated** to an almost desperate effort to fill up the empty midday hours.

12 "Let's go see can we find some locusts on the hill," someone suggested.

13 Joey was scornful. "Ain't no more locusts there. Y'all got 'em all while they was still green."

14 The argument that followed was brief and not really worth the effort. Hunting locust trees wasn't fun anymore by now.

15 "Tell you what," said Joey finally, his eyes sparkling. "Let's us go over to Miss Lottie's."

16 The idea caught on at once, for annoying Miss Lottie was always fun. I was still child enough to scamper along with the group over rickety fences and through bushes that tore our already raggedy clothes, back to where Miss Lottie lived. I think now that we must have made a tragicomic spectacle, five or six kids of different ages, each of us clad in only one garment—the girls in faded dresses that were too long or too short, the boys in patchy pants, their sweaty brown chests gleaming in the hot sun. A little cloud of dust followed our thin legs and bare feet as we tramped over the barren land.

17 When Miss Lottie's house came into view we stopped, ostensibly to plan our strategy, but actually to reinforce our courage. Miss Lottie's house was the most ramshackle of all our ramshackle homes. The sun and rain had long since faded its rickety frame siding from white to a sullen gray. The boards themselves seemed to remain upright not from being nailed together but rather from leaning together, like a house that a child might have constructed from cards. A brisk wind might have blown it down, and the fact that it was still standing implied a kind of enchantment that was stronger than the elements. There it stood and as far as I know is standing yet—a gray, rotting thing with no porch, no shutters, no steps, set on a cramped lot with no grass, not even any weeds—a monument to decay.

18 In front of the house in a squeaky rocking chair sat Miss Lottie's son, John Burke, completing the impression of decay. John Burke was what was known as queer-headed. Black and ageless, he sat rocking day in and day out in a

Please note that excerpts and passages in the StudySync® library and this workbook are intended as touchstones to generate interest in an author's work. The excerpts and passages do not substitute for the reading of entire texts, and StudySync® strongly recommends that students seek out and purchase the whole literary or informational work in order to experience it as the author intended. Links to online resellers are available in our digital library. In addition, complete works may be ordered through an authorized reseller by filling out and returning to StudySync® the order form enclosed in this workbook.

Reading & Writing Companion   7

mindless stupor, lulled by the monotonous squeak-squawk of the chair. A battered hat atop his shaggy head shaded him from the sun. Usually John Burke was totally unaware of everything outside his quiet dream world. But if you disturbed him, if you intruded upon his fantasies, he would become enraged, strike out at you, and curse at you in some strange enchanted language which only he could understand. We children made a game of thinking of ways to disturb John Burke and then to elude his violent retribution.

19 But our real fun and our real fear lay in Miss Lottie herself. Miss Lottie seemed to be at least a hundred years old. Her big frame still held traces of the tall, powerful woman she must have been in youth, although it was now bent and drawn. Her smooth skin was a dark reddish brown, and her face had Indian-like features and the stern **stoicism** that one associates with Indian faces. Miss Lottie didn't like intruders either, especially children. She never left her yard, and nobody ever visited her. We never knew how she managed those necessities which depend on human interaction—how she ate, for example, or even whether she ate. When we were tiny children, we thought Miss Lottie was a witch and we made up tales that we half believed ourselves about her exploits. We were far too sophisticated now, of course, to believe the witch nonsense. But old fears have a way of clinging like cobwebs, and so when we sighted the tumbledown shack, we had to stop to reinforce our nerves.

20 "Look, there she is," I whispered, forgetting that Miss Lottie could not possibly have heard me from that distance. "She's fooling with them crazy flowers."

21 "Yeh, look at 'er."

22 Miss Lottie's marigolds were perhaps the strangest part of the picture. Certainly they did not fit in with the crumbling decay of the rest of her yard. Beyond the dusty brown yard, in front of the sorry gray house, rose suddenly and shockingly a dazzling strip of bright blossoms, clumped together in enormous mounds, warm and passionate and sun-golden. The old black witch-woman worked on them all summer, every summer, down on her creaky knees, weeding and cultivating and arranging, while the house crumbled and John Burke rocked. For some perverse reason, we children hated those marigolds. They interfered with the perfect ugliness of the place; they were too beautiful; they said too much that we could not understand; they did not make sense. There was something in the vigor with which the old woman destroyed the weeds that intimidated us. It should have been a comical sight—the old woman with the man's hat on her cropped white head, leaning over the bright mounds, her big backside in the air—but it wasn't comical, it was something we could not name. We had to annoy her by whizzing a pebble into her flowers or by yelling a dirty word, then dancing away from her rage, reveling in our youth and mocking her age. Actually, I think it was the

flowers we wanted to destroy, but nobody had the nerve to try it, not even Joey, who was usually fool enough to try anything.

23 "Y'all git some stones," commanded Joey now and was met with instant giggling obedience as everyone except me began to gather pebbles from the dusty ground. "Come on, Lizabeth."

24 I just stood there peering through the bushes, torn between wanting to join the fun and feeling that it was all a bit silly.

25 "You scared, Lizabeth?"

26 I cursed and spat on the ground—my favorite gesture of phony bravado. "Y'all children get the stones, I'll show you how to use 'em."

27 I said before that we children were not consciously aware of how thick were the bars of our cage. I wonder now, though, whether we were not more aware of it than I thought. Perhaps we had some dim notion of what we were, and how little chance we had of being anything else. Otherwise, why would we have been so preoccupied with destruction? Anyway, the pebbles were collected quickly, and everybody looked at me to begin the fun.

28 "Come on, y'all."

29 We crept to the edge of the bushes that bordered the narrow road in front of Miss Lottie's place. She was working placidly, kneeling over the flowers, her dark hand plunged into the golden mound. Suddenly *zing*—an expertly aimed stone cut the head off one of the blossoms.

30 "Who out there?" Miss Lottie's backside came down and her head came up as her sharp eyes searched the bushes. "You better git!"

31 We had crouched down out of sight in the bushes, where we stifled the giggles that insisted on coming. Miss Lottie gazed warily across the road for a moment, then cautiously returned to her weeding. *Zing*—Joey sent a pebble into the blooms, and another marigold was beheaded.

32 Miss Lottie was enraged now. She began struggling to her feet, leaning on a rickety cane and shouting. "Y'all git! Go on home!" Then the rest of the kids let loose with their pebbles, storming the flowers and laughing wildly and senselessly at Miss Lottie's impotent rage. She shook her stick at us and started shakily toward the road crying, "Git 'long! John Burke! John Burke, come help!"

33 Then I lost my head entirely, mad with the power of inciting such rage, and ran out of the bushes in the storm of pebbles, straight toward Miss Lottie,

Please note that excerpts and passages in the StudySync® library and this workbook are intended as touchstones to generate interest in an author's work. The excerpts and passages do not substitute for the reading of entire texts, and StudySync® strongly recommends that students seek out and purchase the whole literary or informational work in order to experience it as the author intended. Links to online resellers are available in our digital library. In addition, complete works may be ordered through an authorized reseller by filling out and returning to StudySync® the order form enclosed in this workbook.

Reading & Writing
Companion

9

chanting madly, "Old witch, fell in a ditch, picked up a penny and thought she was rich!" The children screamed with delight, dropped their pebbles, and joined the crazy dance, swarming around Miss Lottie like bees and chanting, "Old lady witch!" while she screamed curses at us. The madness lasted only a moment, for John Burke, startled at last, lurched out of his chair, and we dashed for the bushes just as Miss Lottie's cane went whizzing at my head.

34   I did not join the merriment when the kids gathered again under the oak in our bare yard.

35   Suddenly I was ashamed, and I did not like being ashamed. The child in me sulked and said it was all in fun, but the woman in me flinched at the thought of the **malicious** attack that I had led. The mood lasted all afternoon. When we ate the beans and rice that was supper that night, I did not notice my father's silence, for he was always silent these days, nor did I notice my mother's absence, for she always worked until well into evening. Joey and I had a particularly bitter argument after supper; his exuberance got on my nerves. Finally I stretched out upon the pallet in the room we shared and fell into a fitful doze. When I awoke, somewhere in the middle of the night, my mother had returned, and I vaguely listened to the conversation that was audible through the thin walls that separated our rooms. At first I heard no words, only voices. My mother's voice was like a cool, dark room in summer— peaceful, soothing, quiet. I loved to listen to it; it made things seem all right somehow. But my father's voice cut through hers, shattering the peace.

36   "Twenty-two years, Maybelle, twenty-two years," he was saying, "and I got nothing for you, nothing, nothing."

37   "It's all right, honey, you'll get something. Everybody out of work now, you know that."

38   "It ain't right. Ain't no man ought to eat his woman's food year in and year out, and see his children running wild. Ain't nothing right about that."

39   "Honey, you took good care of us when you had it. Ain't nobody got nothing nowadays."

40   "I ain't talking about nobody else, I'm talking about *me*. God knows I try." My mother said something I could not hear, and my father cried out louder, "What must a man do, tell me that?"

41   "Look, we ain't starving. I git paid every week, and Mrs. Ellis is real nice about giving me things. She gonna let me have Mr. Ellis's old coat for you this winter—"

42   "Damn Mr. Ellis's coat! And damn his money! You think I want white folks' leavings?

43   "Damn, Maybelle"—and suddenly he sobbed, loudly and painfully, and cried helplessly and hopelessly in the dark night. I had never heard a man cry before. I did not know men ever cried. I covered my ears with my hands but could not cut off the sound of my father's harsh, painful, despairing sobs. My father was a strong man who could whisk a child upon his shoulders and go singing through the house. My father whittled toys for us, and laughed so loud that the great oak seemed to laugh with him, and taught us how to fish and hunt rabbits. How could it be that my father was crying? But the sobs went on, unstifled, finally quieting until I could hear my mother's voice, deep and rich, humming softly as she used to hum to a frightened child.

44   The world had lost its boundary lines. My mother, who was small and soft, was now the strength of the family; my father, who was the rock on which the family had been built, was sobbing like the tiniest child. Everything was suddenly out of tune, like a broken accordion. Where did I fit into this crazy picture? I do not now remember my thoughts, only a feeling of great bewilderment and fear.

45   Long after the sobbing and humming had stopped, I lay on the pallet, still as stone with my hands over my ears, wishing that I too could cry and be comforted. The night was silent now except for the sound of the crickets and of Joey's soft breathing. But the room was too crowded with fear to allow me to sleep, and finally, feeling the terrible aloneness of 4 A.M., I decided to awaken Joey.

46   "Ouch! What's the matter with you? What you want?" he demanded disagreeably when I had pinched and slapped him awake.

47   "Come on, wake up."

48   "What for? Go 'way."

49   I was lost for a reasonable reply. I could not say, "I'm scared and I don't want to be alone," so I merely said, "I'm going out. If you want to come, come on."

50   The promise of adventure awoke him. "Going out now? Where to, Lizabeth? What you going to do?"

51   I was pulling my dress over my head. Until now I had not thought of going out. "Just come on," I replied tersely.

52   I was out the window and halfway down the road before Joey caught up with me.

53 "Wait, Lizabeth, where you going?"

54 I was running as if the Furies were after me, as perhaps they were—running silently and furiously until I came to where I had half known I was headed: to Miss Lottie's yard.

55 The half-dawn light was more eerie than complete darkness, and in it the old house was like the ruin that my world had become—foul and crumbling, a grotesque caricature. It looked haunted, but I was not afraid, because I was haunted too.

56 "Lizabeth, you lost your mind?" panted Joey.

57 I had indeed lost my mind, for all the smoldering emotions of that summer swelled in me and burst—the great need for my mother who was never there, the hopelessness of our poverty and degradation, the bewilderment of being neither child nor woman and yet both at once, the fear unleashed by my father's tears. And these feelings combined in one great impulse toward destruction.

58 "Lizabeth!"

59 I leaped furiously into the mounds of marigolds and pulled madly, trampling and pulling and destroying the perfect yellow blooms. The fresh smell of early morning and of dew-soaked marigolds spurred me on as I went tearing and mangling and sobbing while Joey tugged my dress or my waist crying, "Lizabeth, stop, please stop!"

60 And then I was sitting in the ruined little garden among the uprooted and ruined flowers, crying and crying, and it was too late to undo what I had done. Joey was sitting beside me, silent and frightened, not knowing what to say. Then, "Lizabeth, look!'

61 I opened my swollen eyes and saw in front of me a pair of large, calloused feet; my gaze lifted to the swollen legs, the age-distorted body clad in a tight cotton nightdress, and then the shadowed Indian face surrounded by stubby white hair. And there was no rage in the face now, now that the garden was destroyed and there was nothing any longer to be protected.

62 "M-miss Lottie!" I scrambled to my feet and just stood there and stared at her, and that was the moment when childhood faded and womanhood began. That violent, crazy act was the last act of childhood. For as I gazed at the immobile face with the sad, weary eyes, I gazed upon a kind of reality which is hidden to childhood. The witch was no longer a witch but only a broken old woman who had dared to create beauty in the midst of ugliness and sterility. She had been born in squalor and lived in it all her life. Now at the end of that

NOTES

life she had nothing except a falling down hut, a wrecked body, and John Burke, the mindless son of her passion. Whatever verve there was left in her, whatever was of love and beauty and joy that had not been squeezed out by life, had been there in the marigolds she had so tenderly cared for.

63 Of course I could not express the things that I knew about Miss Lottie as I stood there awkward and ashamed. The years have put words to the things I knew in that moment, and as I look back upon it, I know that that moment marked the end of innocence. Innocence involves an unseeing acceptance of things at face value, an ignorance of the area below the surface. In that humiliating moment I looked beyond myself and into the depths of another person. This was the beginning of **compassion**, and one cannot have both compassion and innocence.

64 The years have taken me worlds away from that time and that place, from the dust and squalor of our lives, and from the bright thing that I destroyed in a blind, childish striking out at God knows what. Miss Lottie died long ago and many years have passed since I last saw her hut, completely barren at last, for despite my wild contrition she never planted marigolds again. Yet, there are times when the image of those passionate yellow mounds returns with a painful poignancy. For one does not have to be ignorant and poor to find that his life is as barren as the dusty yards of our town. And I too have planted marigolds.

© 1994 by Eugenia Collier, Breeder and Other Stories. Reproduced by permission of Eugenia Collier. Originally published in the *Negro Digest*, November, 1969.

 THINK QUESTIONS CA-CCSS: CA.RL.9-10.1, CA.RL.9-10.3, CA.L.9-10.4a, CA.L.9-10.4b, CA.L.9-10.4d

1. How do we know that Lizabeth is on the verge of becoming an adult? Refer to several details from the text.

2. Citing details from the text, how do you think Lizabeth's destruction of Miss Lottie's marigolds relates to her transition from adolescence to adulthood?

3. What does the narrator mean in paragraph 7 when she says, "...these days are ill-defined in my memory, running together and combining like a fresh watercolor painting left out in the rain"? What type of literary device is the author using here? Provide examples from the text to support your answer.

4. Use context to determine the meaning of the word **prosperity** as it is used in *Marigolds*. Write your definition of "prosperity" here and tell how you got it.

5. Remembering that the Latin root *mal* means "evil," and the suffix *-ious* means "full of," use the context clues provided in the passage to determine the meaning of **malicious.** Write your definition of "malicious" and tell how you determined it.

CLOSE READ

CA-CCSS: CA.RL.9-10.1, CA.RL.9-10.2, CA.RL.9-10.3, CA.RL.9-10.4, CA.W.9-10.4, CA.W.9-10.5, CA.W.9-10.6, CA.W.9-10.9a, CA.W.9-10.10, CA.L.9-10.4b

Reread the short story "Marigolds." As you reread, complete the Focus Questions below. Then use your answers and annotations from the questions to help you complete the Writing Prompt.

 FOCUS QUESTIONS

1. As you reread *Marigolds,* identify important details that reveal Lizabeth's character, especially from the middle of the story to the end. What makes her a complex character? Highlight textual evidence and make annotations to show how the details reveal Lizabeth's complexity.

2. One of the ways an author develops a character is by describing how the character interacts with the setting. The narrator provides many details about the setting in the early part of the story. How does Lizabeth feel about her town? Highlight textual evidence and annotate to explain the effect the setting has on Lizabeth, and how she interacts with the setting.

3. An author will sometimes use figurative language to develop a reader's understanding of a character and the setting. When Lizabeth begins to describe Miss Lottie's house in paragraph 17, she uses a simile, saying it is "like a house that a child might have constructed from cards." How do images like this help the reader understand Miss Lottie's situation? Highlight other descriptions of Miss Lottie and her house. Annotate to explain how these details help develop the ideas and advance the events in the story.

4. One way that authors develop complex characters is by showing how they interact with other characters. In paragraph 16, how does Lizabeth react when Joey suggests that they all go to Miss Lottie's house? How does Lizabeth feel later that afternoon as a result? Find evidence in the text to explain why Lizabeth does not join in the group's "merriment" when they return home.

5. What in Lizabeth's life causes her to see Miss Lottie as an antagonist? Highlight textual evidence to help explain your ideas. How does Lizabeth deal with her rage against Miss Lottie? How does this action affect Lizabeth at the time and later, when she narrates the story? Identify details and explain how Lizabeth changes from the beginning of the story. Explain the role empathy plays in her changes. How do these elements help to express the story's central idea, or theme?

6. Consider the word *vividly,* from the last sentence in paragraph 2 of *Marigolds.* What is the affix of this word? What is the word's root? Is the root a base word, meaning that it can stand alone as a word? Use context and what you know about the affix and root to guess at the meaning of *vividly.* Now use a good dictionary or search online to find out the etymology, or origin, of *vividly.* Finally, write as many other words you can think of that are in the same family, or share the same root, as *vividly.*

WRITING PROMPT

In *Marigolds,* a grown-up Lizabeth tells a story about her adolescence from the perspective of her adult self. Analyze the character of Lizabeth, both as an adolescent and an adult. Which key words and phrases that the author uses best describe Lizabeth's changing character? How does Lizabeth's adolescence affect her decisions and actions in the story? Identify specific textual details that show this. How can we tell that the adult Lizabeth has learned something from this experience? Be sure to use textual evidence in your response.

Please note that excerpts and passages in the StudySync® library and this workbook are intended as touchstones to generate interest in an author's work. The excerpts and passages do not substitute for the reading of entire texts, and StudySync® strongly recommends that students seek out and purchase the whole literary or informational work in order to experience it as the author intended. Links to online resellers are available in our digital library. In addition, complete works may be ordered through an authorized reseller by filling out and returning to StudySync® the order form enclosed in this workbook.

Reading & Writing Companion **15**

TO KILL A MOCKINGBIRD

FICTION
Harper Lee
1960

INTRODUCTION

Drawing from events in her own childhood, Harper Lee completed *To Kill A Mockingbird* just prior to the peak of the Civil Rights Movement. It created an immediate sensation, winning the Pulitzer Prize in 1961 and selling over fifteen million copies. Told through the eyes of a six-year old girl growing up in Alabama during the Great Depression, Lee's novel is renowned for its warmth and humor, despite dealing with the serious issue of racial injustice. In this excerpt, Scout, the narrator, learns a lesson about compassion.

"You never really understand a person until...you climb into his skin and walk around in it."

 FIRST READ

 NOTES

Excerpt from Chapter 3

1   Walter looked as if he had been raised on fish food: his eyes, as blue as Dill Harris's, were red-rimmed and watery. There was no color in his face except at the tip of his nose, which was moistly pink. He fingered the straps of his overalls, nervously picking at the metal hooks.

2   Jem suddenly grinned at him. "Come on home to dinner with us, Walter," he said. "We'd be glad to have you."

3   Walter's face brightened, then darkened.

4   Jem said, "Our daddy's a friend of your daddy's. Scout here, she's crazy—she won't fight you any more."

5   "I wouldn't be too certain of that," I said. Jem's free dispensation of my pledge irked me, but precious noontime minutes were ticking away. "Yeah Walter, I won't jump on you again. Don't you like butterbeans? Our Cal's a real good cook."

6   Walter stood where he was, biting his lip. Jem and I gave up, and we were nearly to the Radley Place when Walter called, "Hey, I'm comin'!"

7   When Walter caught up with us, Jem made pleasant conversation with him. "A **hain't** lives there," he said cordially, pointing to the Radley house. "Ever hear about him, Walter?"

8   "Reckon I have," said Walter. "Almost died first year I come to school and et them pecans—folks say he pizened 'em and put 'em over on the school side of the fence."

9 Jem seemed to have little fear of Boo Radley now that Walter and I walked beside him. Indeed, Jem grew boastful: "I went all the way up to the house once," he said to Walter.

10 "Anybody who went up to the house once oughta not to still run every time he passes it," I said to the clouds above.

11 "And who's runnin', Miss Priss?"

12 "You are, when ain't anybody with you."

13 By the time we reached our front steps Walter had forgotten he was a Cunningham. Jem ran to the kitchen and asked Calpurnia to set an extra plate, we had company.

...

14 After supper, Atticus sat down with the paper and called, "Scout, ready to read?" The Lord sent me more than I could bear, and I went to the front porch. Atticus followed me.

15 "Something wrong, Scout?"

16 I told Atticus I didn't feel very well and didn't think I'd go to school any more if it was all right with him.

17 Atticus sat down in the swing and crossed his legs. His fingers wandered to his watchpocket; he said that was the only way he could think. He waited in **amiable** silence, and I sought to reinforce my position: "You never went to school and you do all right, so I'll just stay home too. You can teach me like Granddaddy taught you 'n' Uncle Jack."

18 "No I can't," said Atticus. "I have to make a living. Besides, they'd put me in jail if I kept you at home—dose of **magnesia** for you tonight and school tomorrow."

19 "I'm feeling all right, really."

20 "Thought so. Now what's the matter?"

21 Bit by bit, I told him the day's misfortunes. "—and she said you taught me all wrong, so we can't ever read any more, ever. Please don't send me back, please sir."

22 Atticus stood up and walked to the end of the porch. When he completed his examination of the **wisteria** vine he strolled back to me.

23   "First of all," he said, "if you can learn a simple trick, Scout, you'll get along a lot better with all kinds of folks. You never really understand a person until you consider things from his point of view—"

24   "Sir?"

25   "—until you climb into his skin and walk around in it."

Excerpt from Chapter 15

26   I looked around the crowd. It was a summer's night, but the men were dressed, most of them, in overalls and denim shirts buttoned up to the collars. I thought they must be cold-natured, as their sleeves were unrolled and buttoned at the cuffs. Some wore hats pulled firmly down over their ears. They were sullen-looking, sleepy-eyed men who seemed unused to late hours. I sought once more for a familiar face, and at the center of the semi-circle I found one.

27   "Hey, Mr. Cunningham."

28   The man did not hear me, it seemed.

29   "Hey, Mr. Cunningham. How's your **entailment** getting' along?"

30   Mr. Walter Cunningham's legal affairs were well known to me; Atticus had once described them at length. The big man blinked and hooked his thumbs in his overall straps. He seemed uncomfortable; he cleared his throat and looked away. My friendly overture had fallen flat.

31   Mr. Cunningham wore no hat, and the top half of his forehead was white in contrast to his sunscorched face, which led me to believe that he wore one most days. He shifted his feet, clad in heavy work shoes.

32   "Don't you remember me, Mr. Cunningham? I'm Jean Louise Finch. You brought us some hickory nuts one time, remember?" I began to sense the futility one feels when unacknowledged by a chance acquaintance.

33   "I go to school with Walter," I began again. "He's your boy, ain't he? Ain't he, sir?"

34   Mr. Cunningham was moved to a faint nod. He did know me, after all.

35   "He's in my grade," I said, "and he does right well. He's a good boy," I added, "a real nice boy. We brought him home for dinner one time. Maybe he told you about me, I beat him up one time but he was real nice about it. Tell him hey for me, won't you?"

36 Atticus had said it was the polite thing to talk to people about what they were interested in, not about what you were interested in. Mr. Cunningham displayed no interest in his son, so I tackled his entailment once more in a last-ditch effort to make him feel at home.

37 "Entailments are bad," I was advising him, when I slowly awoke to the fact that I was addressing the entire aggregation. The men were all looking at me, some had their mouths half-open. Atticus had stopped poking at Jem: they were standing together beside Dill. Their attention amounted to fascination. Atticus's mouth, even, was half-open, an attitude he had once described as uncouth. Our eyes met and he shut it.

38 "Well, Atticus, I was just sayin' to Mr. Cunningham that entailments are bad an' all that, but you said not to worry, it takes a long time sometimes . . . that you all'd ride it out together . . ." I was slowly drying up, wondering what idiocy I had committed. Entailments seemed all right enough for livingroom talk.

39 I began to feel sweat gathering at the edges of my hair; I could stand anything but a bunch of people looking at me. They were quite still.

40 "What's the matter?" I asked.

41 Atticus said nothing. I looked around and up at Mr. Cunningham, whose face was equally impassive. Then he did a peculiar thing. He squatted down and took me by both shoulders.

42 "I'll tell him you said hey, little lady," he said.

43 Then he straightened up and waved a big paw. "Let's clear out," he called. "Let's get going, boys."

44 As they had come, in ones and twos the men shuffled back to their ramshackle cars. Doors slammed, engines coughed, and they were gone.

Excerpted from *To Kill a Mockingbird* by Harper Lee, published by Grand Central Publishing.

THINK QUESTIONS CA-CCSS: CA.RL.9-10.1, CA.L.9-10.4a, CA.L.9-10.4d

1. Walter speaks in a Southern dialect that reveals not only where he grew up but also other things about his character. Cite an example of Walter's dialect and explain what it tells about his character.

2. Reread the scene when Atticus asks Scout to read. Write a few sentences describing Scout and Atticus's relationship. Cite details from the text to support your answer.

3. Citing details from the text, write a brief explanation of why Scout is successful in "breaking the spell" in front of the jailhouse.

4. Remembering that the Latin root amicus means "friend," use your knowledge of other sentence parts and context clues provided in the passage to determine the meaning of the word amiable.

5. What context clues help you determine the meaning of **magnesia** as it is used in the passage? Write your definition of "magnesia" here and explain which context clues helped you determine its meaning and how they did so.

CLOSE READ

CA-CCSS: CA.RL.9-10.1, CA.RL.9-10.3, CA.RL.9-10.4, CA.W.9-10.4, CA.W.9-10.5, CA.W.9-10.6, CA.W.9-10.9a, CA.W.9-10.10

Reread the excerpts from *To Kill a Mockingbird*. As you reread, complete the Focus Questions below. Then use your answers and annotations from the questions to help you complete the Writing Prompt.

FOCUS QUESTIONS

1. In paragraphs 1–5 of the excerpt, what can you infer about Jem and Scout's relationship? What is Scout's reaction to Jem's behavior? Highlight textual evidence and make annotations to support your analysis of the relationship between these two characters.

2. Authors can develop characters through dialogue, or the conversations among the characters. How is the language Jem, Scout, and Walter use similar? How does Walter speak differently than Jem and Scout? How does dialect help develop the characters and enhance the story? Cite textual evidence to support your analysis.

3. Inferences based on textual evidence can support an interpretation or analysis as powerfully as evidence that is explicitly stated. What can you infer about how well or poorly Atticus understands Scout from his reaction to her request to stay home from school the next day? What can you infer about their relationship as a result of this moment? Highlight your evidence and annotate to explain your answer.

4. When Scout attempts to engage Mr. Cunningham in conversation, what can you infer about her? Highlight textual evidence to show how this gesture connects to Atticus's advice about dealing with others. How does Scout feel about her attempts at conversation with Mr. Cunningham? Cite textual evidence to explain.

5. Sometimes you must make an inference about the meaning of a text from a single statement or action of one of the characters. Understanding why a character says something or does something should be evaluated in light of the context of the situation and the motivations of the character. In paragraph 42, Mr. Cunningham says to Scout, "I'll tell him you said hey, little lady." What can you infer about Mr. Cunningham based on this dialogue? What subsequent plot event offers explicit evidence of your inference about the meaning of Mr. Cunningham's statement?

6. Examine the role empathy plays in each of these excerpts. How does Atticus try to instill the idea of empathy in Scout? How do other characters display, or try to display, empathy? Highlight evidence from the text to support your explanation.

WRITING PROMPT

In Chapter 15 of *To Kill a Mockingbird,* lawyer Atticus Finch is at a jailhouse protecting his client, Tom Robinson, an African American man accused of attacking a white woman in their Alabama town, from a lynch mob. In at least 300 words, explain how Scout's actions dispel the tension of the situation. How do the events that unfold in this scene relate to the theme of compassion developed in other sections of the excerpted novel? Cite textual evidence to support your inferences and analysis.

Please note that excerpts and passages in the StudySync® library and this workbook are intended as touchstones to generate interest in an author's work. The excerpts and passages do not substitute for the reading of entire texts, and StudySync® strongly recommends that students seek out and purchase the whole literary or informational work in order to experience it as the author intended. Links to online resellers are available in our digital library. In addition, complete works may be ordered through an authorized reseller by filling out and returning to StudySync® the order form enclosed in this workbook.

Reading & Writing
Companion

23

THE JUNGLE

FICTION
Upton Sinclair
1906

INTRODUCTION

For seven weeks, Upton Sinclair worked side-by-side with new immigrants in Chicago's meatpacking district to research his groundbreaking book, *The Jungle*. Considered a cornerstone of Marxist literature, his searing exposé of the dismal conditions in factories and the horrors of the industry itself led Theodore Roosevelt to call him a muckracker, but eventually paved the way to the passage of The Meat Inspection Act and The Pure Food and Drug Act of 1906. In this passage, new workers get their first taste of Chicago and the stockyards.

"They were tied to the great packing machine, and tied to it for life."

 FIRST READ

Excerpt from Chapter 2

1   It was in the **stockyards** that Jonas' friend had gotten rich, and so to Chicago the party was bound. They knew that one word, Chicago and that was all they needed to know, at least, until they reached the city. Then, tumbled out of the cars without ceremony, they were no better off than before; they stood staring down the vista of Dearborn Street, with its big black buildings towering in the distance, unable to realize that they had arrived, and why, when they said "Chicago," people no longer pointed in some direction, but instead looked **perplexed**, or laughed, or went on without paying any attention. They were pitiable in their helplessness; above all things they stood in deadly terror of any sort of person in official uniform, and so whenever they saw a policeman they would cross the street and hurry by. For the whole of the first day they wandered about in the midst of deafening confusion, utterly lost; and it was only at night that, cowering in the doorway of a house, they were finally discovered and taken by a policeman to the station. In the morning an interpreter was found, and they were taken and put upon a car, and taught a new word—"stockyards." Their delight at discovering that they were to get out of this adventure without losing another share of their possessions it would not be possible to describe.

2   They sat and stared out of the window. They were on a street which seemed to run on forever, mile after mile—thirty-four of them, if they had known it—and each side of it one uninterrupted row of wretched little two-story frame buildings. Down every side street they could see, it was the same—never a hill and never a hollow, but always the same endless vista of ugly and dirty little wooden buildings. Here and there would be a bridge crossing a filthy creek, with hard-baked mud shores and dingy sheds and docks along it; here and there would be a railroad crossing, with a tangle of switches, and locomotives puffing, and rattling freight cars filing by; here and there would

Please note that excerpts and passages in the StudySync® library and this workbook are intended as touchstones to generate interest in an author's work. The excerpts and passages do not substitute for the reading of entire texts, and StudySync® strongly recommends that students seek out and purchase the whole literary or informational work in order to experience it as the author intended. Links to online resellers are available in our digital library. In addition, complete works may be ordered through an authorized reseller by filling out and returning to StudySync® the order form enclosed in this workbook.

Reading & Writing Companion   **25**

be a great factory, a dingy building with innumerable windows in it, and immense volumes of smoke pouring from the chimneys, darkening the air above and making filthy the earth beneath. But after each of these interruptions, the **desolate** procession would begin again—the procession of dreary little buildings.

3   A full hour before the party reached the city they had begun to note the perplexing changes in the atmosphere. It grew darker all the time, and upon the earth the grass seemed to grow less green. Every minute, as the train sped on, the colors of things became dingier; the fields were grown parched and yellow, the landscape hideous and bare. And along with the thickening smoke they began to notice another circumstance, a strange, pungent odor. They were not sure that it was unpleasant, this odor; some might have called it sickening, but their taste in odors was not developed, and they were only sure that it was curious. Now, sitting in the trolley car, they realized that they were on their way to the home of it—that they had traveled all the way from Lithuania to it. It was now no longer something far off and faint, that you caught in whiffs; you could literally taste it, as well as smell it—you could take hold of it, almost, and examine it at your leisure. They were divided in their opinions about it. It was an elemental odor, raw and crude; it was rich, almost rancid, sensual, and strong. There were some who drank it in as if it were an intoxicant; there were others who put their handkerchiefs to their faces. The new emigrants were still tasting it, lost in wonder, when suddenly the car came to a halt, and the door was flung open, and a voice shouted— "Stockyards!"

Excerpt from Chapter 10

4   In the spring there were cold rains, that turned the streets into canals and bogs; the mud would be so deep that wagons would sink up to the hubs, so that half a dozen horses could not move them. Then, of course, it was impossible for any one to get to work with dry feet; and this was bad for men that were poorly clad and shod, and still worse for women and children. Later came midsummer, with the stifling heat, when the dingy killing beds of Durham's became a very purgatory; one time, in a single day, three men fell dead from sunstroke. All day long the rivers of hot blood poured forth, until, with the sun beating down, and the air motionless, the stench was enough to knock a man over; all the old smells of a generation would be drawn out by this heat—for there was never any washing of the walls and rafters and pillars, and they were caked with the filth of a lifetime. The men who worked on the killing beds would come to reek with foulness, so that you could smell one of them fifty feet away; there was simply no such thing as keeping decent, the most careful man gave it up in the end, and **wallowed** in uncleanness. There was not even a place where a man could wash his hands, and the men ate as much raw blood as food at dinnertime. When they were at work they could

NOTES

not even wipe off their faces—they were as helpless as newly born babes in that respect; and it may seem like a small matter, but when the sweat began to run down their necks and tickle them, or a fly to bother them, it was a torture like being burned alive. Whether it was the slaughterhouses or the dumps that were responsible, one could not say, but with the hot weather there descended upon Packingtown a veritable Egyptian plague of flies; there could be no describing this—the houses would be black with them. There was no escaping; you might provide all your doors and windows with screens, but their buzzing outside would be like the swarming of bees, and whenever you opened the door they would rush in as if a storm of wind were driving them.

5   Perhaps the summertime suggests to you thoughts of the country, visions of green fields and mountains and sparkling lakes. It had no such suggestion for the people in the yards. The great packing machine ground on **remorselessly**, without thinking of green fields; and the men and women and children who were part of it never saw any green thing, not even a flower. Four or five miles to the east of them lay the blue waters of Lake Michigan; but for all the good it did them it might have been as far away as the Pacific Ocean. They had only Sundays, and then they were too tired to walk. They were tied to the great packing machine, and tied to it for life. The managers and superintendents and clerks of Packingtown were all recruited from another class, and never from the workers; they scorned the workers, the very meanest of them. A poor devil of a bookkeeper who had been working in Durham's for twenty years at a salary of six dollars a week, and might work there for twenty more and do no better, would yet consider himself a gentleman, as far removed as the poles from the most skilled worker on the killing beds; he would dress differently, and live in another part of the town, and come to work at a different hour of the day, and in every way make sure that he never rubbed elbows with a laboring man. Perhaps this was due to the repulsiveness of the work; at any rate, the people who worked with their hands were a class apart, and were made to feel it.

Please note that excerpts and passages in the StudySync® library and this workbook are intended as touchstones to generate interest in an author's work. The excerpts and passages do not substitute for the reading of entire texts, and StudySync® strongly recommends that students seek out and purchase the whole literary or informational work in order to experience it as the author intended. Links to online resellers are available in our digital library. In addition, complete works may be ordered through an authorized reseller by filling out and returning to StudySync® the order form enclosed in this workbook.

Reading & Writing Companion   **27**

THINK QUESTIONS CA-CCSS: CA.RL.9-10.1, CA.L.9-10.4a, CA.L.9-10.4b, CA.L.9-10.4d

1. How do we know that "the party" referred to in the opening sentence of the first paragraph has just arrived from another country, and cannot speak English? Cite evidence from the text in your answer.

2. The author describes the scene the party sees out the window as it travels to the stockyards in a car. Citing details from the text, what does the landscape reveal about the living conditions of many people who live in and around Chicago?

3. What does the author mean when he describes the "great packing machine" at the beginning of the last paragraph? What type of literary device is the author using, and what does it add to the tone of the selection, or the attitude the author has toward a subject and his or her audience? Cite textual evidence in your response.

4. Use context to determine the meaning of the word perplexed in the first paragraph of Chapter 2 of *The Jungle*. Explain how you figured out the meaning of the word. Then check your inferred meaning in a print or digital dictionary.

5. The word **remorselessly** is an adverb. The noun remorse, which means a "gnawing" feeling of guilt, comes from the Latin root *remordere*, meaning "to bite again". The suffix -*less* means "without". Using this knowledge, what does the adverb "remorselessly" mean? Check your definition to see if it makes sense in context.

CLOSE READ
CA-CCSS: CA.RL.9-10.1, CA.RL.9-10.2, CA.RL.9-10.4, CA.W.9-10.4, CA.W.9-10.5, CA.W.9-10.6, CA.W.9-10.9a, CA.W.9-10.10

Reread the excerpts from *The Jungle*. As you reread, complete the Focus Questions below. Then use your answers and annotations from the questions to help you complete the Writing Prompt.

FOCUS QUESTIONS

1. As you reread the excerpt of *The Jungle*, keep in mind that the meat-packing industry the narrator describes did not have the regulations that are in place today. The author uses descriptive details to help the reader visualize the horrors of the factory life and the challenges the immigrant workers faced. Provide textual details to show how workers reacted to the conditions at the factory.

2. Highlight three or four images that stand out for you in the excerpt. How might these images be symbolic, or serve to stand for larger ideas or concepts? How do these images contribute to a larger message? Annotate to explain your ideas.

3. How does the narrator function as a tool to communicate a political message, or theme, about this industry? Highlight textual details, including descriptions of the city, the factories, and the working conditions. Add an annotation that states the theme, in a complete sentence, based on the text evidence you have highlighted.

4. Highlight one example from the text of figurative language and one example of language that has positive connotations. Identify your examples and explain how they help the reader better understand the conditions the factory workers endured at that time.

5. Think about the excerpt's narration, details, and theme. Which details does the author use that elicit compassion and empathy from you as a reader? Highlight evidence from the text that will help support your view.

WRITING PROMPT

Reread the excerpt from *The Jungle*, focusing on the last section, where immigrants work in the stockyards. Imagine that you are an immigrant worker on a Sunday night, and you are preparing to go to work on Monday morning. Write a first-person narrative of at least 300 words explaining how you prepare for another week at the stockyard and the meat-packing plant. Use descriptive details to help you develop your narrative and allow the reader to visualize the scene. (Remember that while you are creating your own narrative, your descriptions should be consistent with the world described by Updike in *The Jungle*.) When you have finished, state the theme of your narrative in one sentence.

LIFT EVERY VOICE AND SING

POETRY

James Weldon Johnson
1900

INTRODUCTION

James Weldon Johnson was an American poet and academic, as well as an early civil rights activist. He originally wrote "Lift Every Voice and Sing"— which celebrated the gains of African-Americans since the Civil War and offered hope for the future—as a poem. His brother set it to music, and before long it was known as the "Black National Anthem." By the 1920's, the song was

"We have come over a way that with tears has been watered…"

FIRST READ

1 Lift every voice and sing,
2 Till earth and heaven ring,
3 Ring with the harmonies of Liberty,
4 Let our rejoicing rise
5 High as the list'ning skies,
6 Let it **resound** loud as the rolling sea.
7 Sing a song full of the faith that the dark past has taught us
8 Sing a song full of the hope that the present has brought us
9 Facing the rising sun of our new day begun,
10 Let us march on till victory is won.

11 Stony the road we **trod**
12 Bitter the **chast'ning** rod,
13 Felt in the days when hope unborn had died;
14 Yet with a steady beat
15 Have not our weary feet
16 Come to the place for which our fathers sighed?
17 We have come over a way that with tears has been watered
18 We have come, treading our path thro' the blood of the **slaughtered**,
19 Out from the gloomy past, till now we stand at last
20 Where the white gleam of our bright star is cast.

21 God of our weary years,
22 God of our silent tears,
23 Thou who hast brought us thus far on the way;
24 Thou who hast by Thy might,
25 Led us into the light, Keep us forever in the path, we pray.
26 Lest our feet stray from the places, our God, where we meet Thee,
27 Lest, our hearts drunk with the wine of the world, we forget Thee;
28 Shadowed beneath Thy hand, may we forever stand,
29 True to our God, true to our **native** land.

Please note that excerpts and passages in the StudySync® library and this workbook are intended as touchstones to generate interest in an author's work. The excerpts and passages do not substitute for the reading of entire texts, and StudySync® strongly recommends that students seek out and purchase the whole literary or informational work in order to experience it as the author intended. Links to online resellers are available in our digital library. In addition, complete works may be ordered through an authorized reseller by filling out and returning to StudySync® the order form enclosed in this workbook.

Reading & Writing
Companion

31

THINK QUESTIONS   CA-CCSS: CA.RL.9-10.1, CA.L.9-10.4a, CA.L.9-10.4b

1. Reread the first section of the song. What do you think the song is celebrating? What is the "new day" the songwriter refers to in this section? Cite text evidence to support your inference.

2. Reread the second section of the song. Using textual evidence to support your answer, what can you infer about the journey forward from the "dark past"?

3. What inferences can you make about the role of religion or belief in the lives of the people described by this song? Use text evidence to support your answer.

4. The word "chastening" comes from the Latin root *castus,* meaning "pure." Use this knowledge of the root, along with context clues, to determine the meaning of the word chastening as it is used in the selection. Write your definition of "chastening" here and explain how you got it.

5. Remember that you can use what you know about one word to help you understand other words in the same word family. For example, the Latin prefix *re-* means *again,* and you know that the base word, *sound,* refers to something audible, something that you can hear. What can you infer is the meaning of the word **resounding**? Write your definition here.

CLOSE READ

CA-CCSS: CA.RL.9-10.1, CA.RL.9-10.4, CA.W.9-10.4, CA.W.9-10.5, CA.W.9-10.6, CA.W.9-10.9a, CA.W.9-10.10, CA.L.9-10.5a

Reread the poem "Lift Every Voice and Sing." As you reread, complete the Focus Questions below. Then use your answers and annotations from the questions to help you complete the Writing Prompt.

FOCUS QUESTIONS

1. As you reread the text of "Lift Every Voice and Sing," think about the subject of the song. How does the language change over the course of the song, and how does that change impact the tone? Compare the tone of the first verse to the tone of the second verse. Remember that word choice, sound devices, the song's subject, and the songwriter's point of view all contribute to the tone. Highlight evidence from the text to support your answer.

2. A songwriter can use figurative language to appeal to readers' and listeners' senses and create emotional impact. In the second verse, the songwriter writes, "Where the white gleam of our bright star is cast." What kind of figurative language is being used? What does this image mean, and how does it add to the overall meaning of the verse? What other evidence from the text supports the meaning of the verse?

3. In the third verse, the writer includes the words *Thy, Thou,* and *Thee* for the first time. How would you describe effect of these words on the tone in the final verse? What other words or phrases influence the tone? Highlight textual evidence and annotate to explain your ideas. How does this verse relate to the rest of the song?

4. What does the songwriter mean by the phrase, "drunk with the wine of the world" in the third verse? Explain how the phrase is an example of figurative language. What is the songwriter calling on God's help to avoid? Look at the context of the song lyrics for text evidence to help you explain its meaning. Cite this evidence in your explanation.

5. In the second verse, the songwriter writes, "Bitter the chast'ning rod." Look at the context of the word *chast'ning,* (a short form of "chastening") and the use of the word rod. How does the context of the line in which the word appears help you understand its meaning? What does the songwriter mean by a *chast'ning rod*? How does this choice of words in the song help to develop a reader or listener's empathy for the people being described?

WRITING PROMPT

Think about the title of the song "Lift Every Voice and Sing" by James Weldon Johnson. What is the difference between "Lift Every Voice and Sing" and, for example, "Lift Your Voice and Sing?" How does that affect the appeal of the song? How does the writer use figurative language and tone to explore his subject and create meaning? Write a short literary analysis in which you analyze the tone and language of the song and craft an argument about whether they are effective in expressing the songwriter's meaning. Use what you have learned about finding and citing textual evidence to support your claim and explain your ideas.

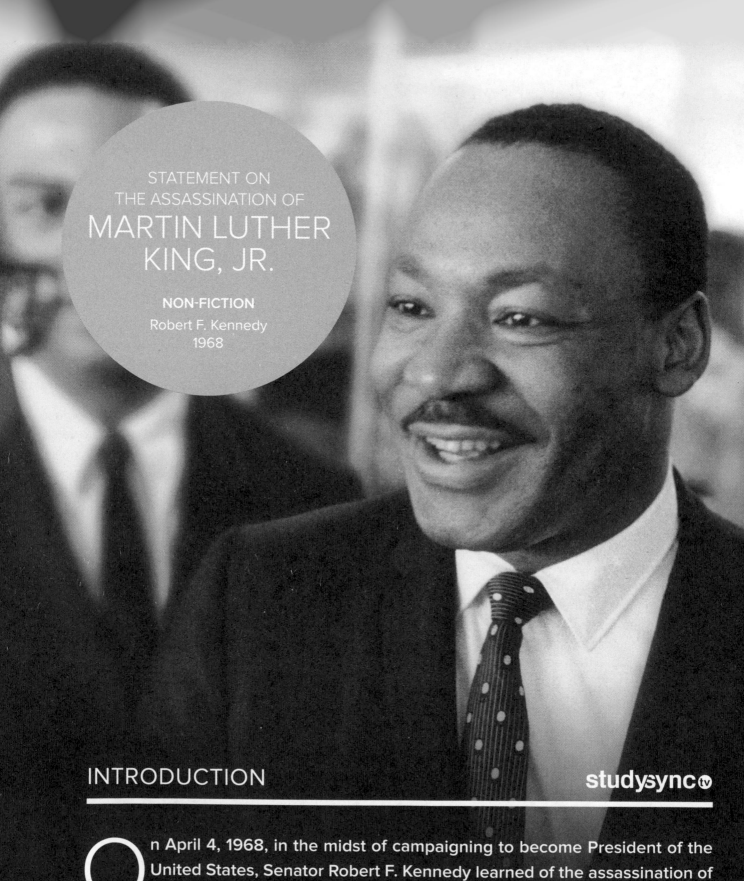

STATEMENT ON
THE ASSASSINATION OF
MARTIN LUTHER KING, JR.

NON-FICTION
Robert F. Kennedy
1968

INTRODUCTION

On April 4, 1968, in the midst of campaigning to become President of the United States, Senator Robert F. Kennedy learned of the assassination of Martin Luther King, Jr. Upon arriving in Indianapolis for a campaign rally, instead of delivering a rousing political speech, Kennedy made some brief but powerful remarks about King's death. During an extremely tense period in American history, Kennedy's speech stands out as an eloquent and passionate

"...what we need in the United States is not violence and lawlessness, but is love..."

FIRST READ

NOTES

1 Ladies and Gentlemen,

2 I'm only going to talk to you just for a minute or so this evening, because I have—some very sad news for all of you—Could you lower those signs, please?—I have some very sad news for all of you, and, I think, sad news for all of our fellow citizens, and people who love peace all over the world; and that is that Martin Luther King was shot and was killed tonight in Memphis, Tennessee.

3 Martin Luther King **dedicated** his life to love and to justice between fellow human beings. He died in the cause of that effort. In this difficult day, in this difficult time for the United States, it's perhaps well to ask what kind of a nation we are and what direction we want to move in. For those of you who are black—considering the evidence evidently is that there were white people who were responsible—you can be filled with bitterness, and with hatred, and a desire for revenge.

4 We can move in that direction as a country, in greater **polarization**—black people amongst blacks, and white amongst whites, filled with hatred toward one another. Or we can make an effort, as Martin Luther King did, to understand, and to comprehend, and replace that violence, that stain of bloodshed that has spread across our land, with an effort to understand, compassion, and love.

5 For those of you who are black and are tempted to fill with—be filled with hatred and mistrust of the injustice of such an act, against all white people, I would only say that I can also feel in my own heart the same kind of feeling. I had a member of my family killed, but he was killed by a white man.

6 But we have to make an effort in the United States. We have to make an effort to understand, to get beyond, or go beyond these rather difficult times.

7   My favorite poem, my—my favorite poet was Aeschylus. And he once wrote:

8   *Even in our sleep, pain which cannot forget*
falls drop by drop upon the heart,
until, in our own despair,
against our will,
comes wisdom
through the awful grace of God.

9   What we need in the United States is not division; what we need in the United States is not hatred; what we need in the United States is not violence and lawlessness, but is love, and wisdom, and compassion toward one another, and a feeling of justice toward those who still suffer within our country, whether they be white or whether they be black.

10 So I ask you tonight to return home, to say a prayer for the family of Martin Luther King—yeah, it's true—but more importantly to say a prayer for our own country, which all of us love—a prayer for understanding and that compassion of which I spoke.

11 We can do well in this country. We will have difficult times. We've had difficult times in the past, but we—and we will have difficult times in the future. It is not the end of violence; it is not the end of lawlessness; and it's not the end of **disorder**.

12 But the vast majority of white people and the vast majority of black people in this country want to live together, want to improve the quality of our life, and want justice for all human beings that **abide** in our land.

13 And let's dedicate ourselves to what the Greeks wrote so many years ago: to tame the **savageness** of man and make gentle the life of this world. Let us dedicate ourselves to that, and say a prayer for our country and for our people.

14 Thank you very much.

THINK QUESTIONS CA-CCSS: CA.RI.9-10.1, CA.L.9-10.4a, CA.L.9-10.4b

1. In the first paragraph of his speech, Kennedy mentions three groups of people that he believes will be saddened by the news of King's assassination. One of them is the audience of listeners in front of him. Who are the other two groups? Support your answer with textual evidence.

2. In the first sentence of the second paragraph, Kennedy briefly explains what made King such an extraordinary figure. What does Kennedy state explicitly, and what can you infer about Kennedy's feelings for Martin Luther King, Jr. from reading his speech? Use details from the text to support your answer.

3. In the third and the fifth paragraphs, Kennedy repeats that Americans have to "make an effort." What does he want Americans to make an effort to do? Use textual evidence to support your answer.

4. Use context clues to determine the meaning of the word **polarization** as it is used in this speech. Write your definition here and explain how you used the context clues to figure out its meaning.

5. The suffix -*ness* added to a word turns it into a noun. Knowing this, use the context clues provided in the .passage to determine the meaning of **savageness.** Write your definition of "savageness" here and explain how you used the context clues to figure out its meaning.

Please note that excerpts and passages in the StudySync® library and this workbook are intended as touchstones to generate interest in an author's work. The excerpts and passages do not substitute for the reading of entire texts, and StudySync® strongly recommends that students seek out and purchase the whole literary or informational work in order to experience it as the author intended. Links to online resellers are available in our digital library. In addition, complete works may be ordered through an authorized reseller by filling out and returning to StudySync® the order form enclosed in this workbook.

Reading & Writing
Companion

37

CLOSE READ
CA-CCSS: CA.RI.9-10.1, CA.RI.9-10.6, CA.RI.9-10.8, CA.W.9-10.4, CA.W.9-10.5, CA.W.9-10.6, CA.W.9-10.9b, CA.W.9-10.10

Reread the text "Statement on the Assassination of Martin Luther King, Jr." As you reread, complete the Focus Questions below. Then use your answers and annotations from the questions to help you complete the Writing Prompt.

 FOCUS QUESTIONS

1. Reread paragraphs 1 and 2. How does Kennedy reveal his point of view about Martin Luther King, Jr. to the audience? Highlight evidence of his point of view in the text and use the annotation tool to explain how his point of view is revealed in the sentences you've chosen.

2. In paragraph 2, Kennedy introduces his argument with a specific claim. Highlight the claim he makes in this paragraph. Also highlight Kennedy's reasons for suggesting that some people might be tempted to take revenge in response to King's death. Do his reasons for this assumption seem valid? Use the annotation tool to explain why or why not.

3. Reread paragraph 3 and highlight places in the text where Kennedy uses the rhetorical devices of repetition and figurative language. What is he trying to emphasize through their use? Use the annotation tool to explain how his language reveals and communicates his purpose and point of view.

4. Kennedy states that he's only going to speak for a few minutes. He later asks his audience to go home and say two prayers, and he repeats the recommendation to say a prayer in his last paragraph. What is his purpose in recommending prayer? Highlight the specific prayers he suggests. Use the annotation tool to explain why you think he suggests prayer. Support your answer with textual evidence.

5. What types of evidence does Kennedy use to elicit empathy from the audience? Do you think the evidence is relevant and sufficient to support Kennedy's specific claims about the pain of loss? Highlight and summarize four instances in which Kennedy supports his claims with evidence. Use the annotation tool to identify the types of evidence and explain whether Kennedy's reasoning based on the evidence elicits empathy from the reader.

WRITING PROMPT

How effectively does Robert F. Kennedy develop his argument in *Statement on the Assassination of Martin Luther King, Jr.*? Does he support his claims with strong evidence? Does his rhetoric successfully communicate his purpose and point of view? Use your understanding of argument, claim, persuasion, author's purpose, and author's point of view to summarize Kennedy's argument and to evaluate whether or not it is persuasive. Support your writing with evidence from the text.

Please note that excerpts and passages in the StudySync® library and this workbook are intended as touchstones to generate interest in an author's work. The excerpts and passages do not substitute for the reading of entire texts, and StudySync® strongly recommends that students seek out and purchase the whole literary or informational work in order to experience it as the author intended. Links to online resellers are available in our digital library. In addition, complete works may be ordered through an authorized reseller by filling out and returning to StudySync® the order form enclosed in this workbook.

Reading & Writing
Companion

39

THE HARVEST GYPSIES

NON-FICTION

John Steinbeck

1936

WHAT HURTS BUSIN

HURTS ME

NATION'S BUSINESS
MAGAZINE

INTRODUCTION

n 1936, John Steinbeck wrote a series of seven articles, "The Harvest Gypsies," for a San Francisco newspaper. The series was later compiled into a short book that reported on the situation of unemployed migrants who were flooding into California, looking for jobs as agricultural workers. This excerpt from the second article in the series details the wretched living conditions that families were forced

"Dignity is all gone, and spirit has turned to sullen anger before it dies."

FIRST READ

Excerpt from Article II

1   This is a family of six; a man, his wife and four children. They live in a tent the color of the ground. Rot has set in on the canvas so that the flaps and the sides hang in tatters and are held together with bits of rusty baling wire. There is one bed in the family and that is a big **tick** lying on the ground inside the tent.

2   They have one quilt and a piece of canvas for bedding. The sleeping arrangement is clever. Mother and father lie down together and two children lie between them. Then, heading the other way; the other two children lie, the littler ones. If the mother and father sleep with their legs spread wide, there is room for the legs of the children.

3   There is more filth here. The tent is full of flies clinging to the apple box that is the dinner table, buzzing about the foul clothes of the children, particularly the baby; who has not been bathed nor cleaned for several days.

4   This family has been on the road longer than the builder of the paper house. There is no toilet here, but there is a clump of willows nearby where human feces lie exposed to the flies—the same flies that are in the tent.

5   Two weeks ago there was another child, a four year old boy. For a few weeks they had noticed that he was kind of lackadaisical, that his eyes had been feverish.

6   They had given him the best place in the bed, between father and mother. But one night he went into convulsions and died, and the next morning the coroner's wagon took him away. It was one step down.

7   They know pretty well that it was a diet of fresh fruit, beans and little else that caused his death. He had no milk for months. With this death there came a

Please note that excerpts and passages in the StudySync® library and this workbook are intended as touchstones to generate interest in an author's work. The excerpts and passages do not substitute for the reading of entire texts, and StudySync® strongly recommends that students seek out and purchase the whole literary or informational work in order to experience it as the author intended. Links to online resellers are available in our digital library. In addition, complete works may be ordered through an authorized reseller by filling out and returning to StudySync® the order form enclosed in this workbook.

Reading & Writing
Companion

41

change of mind in his family. The father and mother now feel that paralyzed dullness with which the mind protects itself against too much sorrow and too much pain.

8   And this father will not be able to make a maximum of four hundred dollars a year any more because he is no longer alert; he isn't quick at piece-work, and he is not able to fight clear of the dullness that has settled on him. His spirit is losing **caste** rapidly.

9   The dullness shows in the faces of this family, and in addition there is a **sullenness** that makes them **taciturn**. Sometimes they still start the older children off to school, but the ragged little things will not go; they hide in ditches or wander off by themselves until it is time to go back to the tent, because they are scorned in the school.

10   The better-dressed children shout and jeer, the teachers are quite often impatient with these additions to their duties, and the parents of the "nice" children do not want to have disease carriers in the schools.

11   The father of this family once had a little grocery store and his family lived in back of it so that even the children could wait on the counter. When the drought set in there was no trade for the store any more.

12   This is the middle class of the squatters' camp. In a few months this family will slip down to the lower class.

13   Dignity is all gone, and spirit has turned to sullen anger before it dies.

14   The next door neighbor family of man, wife and three children of from three to nine years of age, have built a house by driving willow branches into the ground and wattling weeds, tin, old paper and strips of carpet against them.

15   A few branches are placed over the top to keep out the noonday sun. It would not turn water at all. There is no bed.

16   Somewhere the family has found a big piece of old carpet. It is on the ground. To go to bed the members of the family lie on the ground and fold the carpet up over them.

17   The three year old child has a gunny sack tied about his middle for clothing. He has the swollen belly caused by **malnutrition**.

18   He sits on the ground in the sun in front of the house, and the little black fruit flies buzz in circles and land on his closed eyes and crawl up his nose until he weakly brushes them away.

19   They try to get at the mucous in the eye-corners. This child seems to have the reactions of a baby much younger. The first year he had a little milk, but he has had none since.

20   He will die in a very short time. The older children may survive. Four nights ago the mother had a baby in the tent, on the dirty carpet. It was born dead, which was just as well because she could not have fed it at the breast; her own diet will not produce milk.

21   After it was born and she had seen that it was dead, the mother rolled over and lay still for two days. She is up today, tottering around. The last baby, born less than a year ago, lived a week. This woman's eyes have the glazed, far-away look of a sleep walker's eyes.

22   She does not wash clothes any more. The drive that makes for cleanliness has been drained out of her and she hasn't the energy. The husband was a **share-cropper** once, but he couldn't make it go. Now he has lost even the desire to talk.

23   He will not look directly at you for that requires will, and will needs strength. He is a bad field worker for the same reason. It takes him a long time to make up his mind, so he is always late in moving and late in arriving in the fields. His top wage, when he can find work now; which isn't often, is a dollar a day.

Excerpted from *The Harvest Gypsies* by John Steinbeck, published by Heyday.

Please note that excerpts and passages in the StudySync® library and this workbook are intended as touchstones to generate interest in an author's work. The excerpts and passages do not substitute for the reading of entire texts, and StudySync® strongly recommends that students seek out and purchase the whole literary or informational work in order to experience it as the author intended. Links to online resellers are available in our digital library. In addition, complete works may be ordered through an authorized reseller by filling out and returning to StudySync® the order form enclosed in this workbook.

Reading & Writing
Companion

43

THINK QUESTIONS   CA-CCSS: CA.RI.9-10.1, CA.L.9-10.4a, CA.L.9-10.4d

1. How would you describe how the death of their four-year-old son set off a disastrous chain of events for the family? Support your answer with evidence from paragraphs 7–9.

2. How does the treatment of the older children at school help you understand that adults can have as much difficulty showing compassion toward others as children do? Support your answer with evidence from the text.

3. The author, John Steinbeck, states in paragraph 12 that this first family about whom he is writing is in "the middle class of the squatters' camp," but that "[i]n a few months this family will slip down to the lower class." What information does the author use to support his prediction? Explain your reasoning with textual evidence.

4. Use context as a clue to determine the meaning of the word **sullenness** as it is used in paragraph 9 of "The Harvest Gypsies." Write your definition of "sullenness" and identify the context clues that helped you define it. Then consult a print or digital dictionary to find the precise meaning of the word.

5. By remembering that the Latin prefix "mal-" means "bad," "harmful," or "inadequate," use the context clues provided in paragraph 17 to determine the meaning of **malnutrition.** Write your definition of "malnutrition" and explain how you figured out its meaning. Then check a print or digital dictionary to confirm your inferred meaning.

CLOSE READ

CA-CCSS: CA.RI.9-10.1, CA.RI.9-10.3, CA.RI.9-10.6, CA.W.9-10.1b, CA.W.9-10.4, CA.W.9-10.5, CA.W.9-10.6, CA.W.9-10.10

Reread the excerpt from *The Harvest Gypsies*. Then use your answers and annotations from the questions to help you complete the Writing Prompt.

FOCUS QUESTIONS

1. How does Steinbeck organize the information he reveals about the first family in the text? How is the family introduced? What does Steinbeck describe first, and what connections does he make between their living conditions and the state of their health? Cite specific textual evidence in your response.

2. In paragraphs 5–6, Steinbeck writes that when the father and mother saw that their four-year-old boy had eyes that were "feverish," they gave "him the best place in the bed. But one night he went into convulsions and died," and "[i]t was one step down." What does Steinbeck mean by the phrase, "one step down"? What comparisons can you make between the first and second families the author describes that explains what he means when he talks about the middle and lower classes of the squatters' camp, and why this tragic event is "one step down"? Support your answer with specific textual evidence.

3. Make connections between what happens to the boy in the "middle class" family and the events that happen as a result. Annotate examples in the text and identify any important transition words or phrases in paragraphs 7–10 that signal interactions between individuals and events.

4. In addition to the actual horror of physical death, Steinbeck describes the stages a family goes through before reaching the lower class, and compares it to a kind of death. Evaluate his claim that falling from middle-class prosperity and self-sufficiency into poverty is a kind of dying. Highlight evidence from the text that supports this idea.

5. In "The Harvest Gypsies" Steinbeck presents facts and information about a historical event in U.S. history—the plight of migrant workers during the Great Depression. He does not use sensational descriptions of the conditions he found in the migrant camps. He also does not give his opinion. What effect does Steinbeck's straightforward expository style have on the level of empathy readers feel for the people he describes? Highlight specific evidence from the text that will support your ideas.

WRITING PROMPT

How does Steinbeck's detached point of view in "The Harvest Gypsies" help you understand the plight of migrant farm workers living in California during the Great Depression of the 1930s? How does his straightforward style of writing convey facts without emotion? By referring to facts and details in the text, write a brief informative/explanatory essay in which you explain what makes Steinbeck's detached point of view and factual style of writing so effective, despite his emotional subject—the hard lives of the migrant workers. As you plan and organize your essay, think about how Steinbeck connects informational text elements—individuals, events, and ideas—to analyze the situation of the farm workers. Cite evidence from the text in your response.

ENDANGERED DREAMS:

THE GREAT DEPRESSION IN CALIFORNIA

NON-FICTION
Kevin Starr
1996

INTRODUCTION

Endangered Dreams covers the years of the Great Depression, when California became the lodestone for thousands of displaced, unemployed Americans. This excerpt tells the story behind one of the most famous photographs in the world: a careworn migrant worker gazing off-camera, surrounded by her children. Dorothea Lange, photographer for the Farm Security Administration, remembers the events that led to the photograph of Florence Thompson in a pea-

"I saw and approached the hungry and desperate mother, as if drawn by a magnet."

FIRST READ

1   Among the photographs Lange forwarded to Washington was one which soon achieved the **stature** of an American masterpiece. Subsequently entitled *Migrant Mother,* Lange's photograph has become not only the best-known image of the 270,000 plus **negatives** assembled by her Resettlement/Farm Security Administration team, but one of the most universally recognized and appreciated photographs of all time.

2   She almost missed taking it. Returning in March 1936 after a month in the field, Lange was heading north to San Francisco past Nipomo. On the side of the road, on a cold wet miserable day, she saw a sign that said "Pea Pickers Camp." She passed it. After all, at her side on the car seat rested a box containing rolls and packs of exposed film. Accompanied by the rhythmic hum of the windshield wipers, she debated over the next twenty miles the pros and cons of returning. In a sudden instinctive decision, she made a U-turn on the empty highway and returned to the pea pickers' camp. "I saw and approached the hungry and desperate mother, as if drawn by a magnet," she later recalled. "I do not remember how I explained my presence or my camera to her, but I do remember she asked me no questions. I made five **exposures**, working closer and closer from the same direction. I did not ask her name or her history. She told me her age, that she was thirty-two. She said that they had been living on frozen vegetables from surrounding fields, and birds that the children killed. She had just sold the tires from her car to buy food. There she sat in that lean-to tent with her children huddled around her, and seemed to know that my pictures might help her, and so she helped me. There was a sort of equality about it."

3   Some critics have made much of the fact that Lange did not learn the woman's name, which was Florence Thompson, taking this as proof of Lange's photographic **detachment**. In the woman and her three children, stranded in a roadside canvas lean-to, such critics suggest, Lange found a subject for her

photographic art: a subject removed in time and circumstances from her prosperous clients in her previous practice; but she approached her nevertheless from a similarly detached **perspective.** The primary subject of *Migrant Mother,* from this perspective, is photography itself. Such a criticism ignores the fact that as soon as Lange returned to San Francisco and developed these Nipomo negatives (there were actually six, not five as she remembered), she rushed with them to George West at the San Francisco *News*, telling him that thousands of pea pickers in Nipomo were starving because of the frozen harvest. West got the story out in both the *News,* using two of Lange's photographs (but not *Migrant Mother*), and over the wires of the United Press. The federal government, meanwhile, rushed in twenty thousand pounds of food to feed the starving pea pickers.

Excerpted from Endangered Dreams: The Great Depression in California by Kevin Starr, published by Oxford University Press.

THINK QUESTIONS   CA-CCSS: CA.RI.9-10.1, CA.L.9-10.4a, CA.L.9-10.4b

1. How did Lange find the woman who was the subject of *Migrant Mother*? Support your answer with specific textual evidence.

2. What inference does Lange make about why the woman cooperated fully without asking any questions? Support your answer with specific textual evidence.

3. Cite textual evidence to explain why some critics have seen *Migrant Mother* as an example of Lange's "photographic detachment." Give at least two reasons for the critics' theory.

4. Use context as a clue to determine the meaning of **stature** as it is used in the first sentence of *Endangered Dreams: The Great Depression in*

California. Write your definition of "stature" and tell how you determined its meaning. Check the inferred meaning in context and then verify it in a print or digital dictionary.

5. By remembering that the Latin suffix -*ment* is a noun-forming suffix, meaning "state or condition of being," we realize that the word **detachment** in the third paragraph is a noun formed from the verb "detach." Use the context clues provided in the third paragraph to determine the meaning of the word "detachment." Write your definition of the word and tell how you figured out its meaning. Consult a print or digital dictionary to determine the precise meaning of the word and to confirm its part of speech.

CLOSE READ

CA-CCSS: CA.RI.9-10.1, CA.RI.9-10.2, CA.RI.9-10.6, CA.RI.9-10.7, CA.W.9-10.4, CA.W.9-10.5, CA.W.9-10.6, CA.W.9-10.9b, CA.W.9-10.10

Reread the excerpt from *Endangered Dreams*. As you reread, complete the Focus Questions below. Then use your answers and annotations from the questions to help you complete the Writing Prompt.

FOCUS QUESTIONS

1. The excerpt *Endangered Dreams: The Great Depression in California* comes from a book of the same title. Which specific details in the excerpt and the photograph *Migrant Mother* depict a key idea of dreams in danger? What inference can you make about the American Dream during this period in U.S. history? Highlight evidence from both the printed text and the photograph to support your inferences, and write annotations to explain your choices.

2. Review each paragraph's central or main idea and supporting details. Ask yourself what these ideas and details explain, describe, and have in common. Notice how, together, they begin to develop and shape one overall central idea. Based on your analysis, write a sentence that states the overall central idea of the excerpt.

3. How would you summarize the selection? What central idea and supporting details would you include? Write a 5-sentence objective summary of the text. Include only the most important details. Use your own words, but do not include your own judgments or opinions.

4. After closely examining the photograph *Migrant Mother*, write a list of at least five details that you notice. Next to each detail, write a check mark if the detail is also mentioned in the printed text. Then use your findings to state and support a claim as to which medium, in your opinion, provides more information about the circumstances under which this family and many migrant workers were living in California during the Great Depression. Be sure to use evidence from both the photograph and the printed text to support your claim.

5. What is the author's point of view, or perspective, on Lange's compassion for others? Cite two or more details that show his perspective. Highlight and annotate evidence that supports your answer.

WRITING PROMPT

What have you learned about the migrant family shown in *Migrant Mother* from closely analyzing the photograph and the printed text about the photograph? After analyzing the information, do you agree or disagree with the idea that Dorothea Lange photographed the woman and her family from a detached perspective? Write an essay that argues for or against the idea that Lange's photograph and the events surrounding it show she was detached, or removed, from her subject. Use details from both mediums—photography and print—to support your claim. Support your writing with clear reasons and relevant evidence from the printed text and the photograph.

Please note that excerpts and passages in the StudySync® library and this workbook are intended as touchstones to generate interest in an author's work. The excerpts and passages do not substitute for the reading of entire texts, and StudySync® strongly recommends that students seek out and purchase the whole literary or informational work in order to experience it as the author intended. Links to online resellers are available in our digital library. In addition, complete works may be ordered through an authorized reseller by filling out and returning to StudySync® the order form enclosed in this workbook.

Reading & Writing Companion

49

THE GRAPES OF WRATH

FICTION

John Steinbeck
1939

INTRODUCTION

American author John Steinbeck frequently featured downtrodden protagonists in his work, and his Pulitzer Prize-winning masterpiece, *The Grapes of Wrath,* was no exception. First published in 1939, the novel chronicles the fictional Joad family's difficult journey from Oklahoma's Dust Bowl to California during the Great Depression. The following excerpt, set in a typical roadside diner along Route 66, is an independent story, inserted into the midst of

"We got a thousan' miles to go, an' we don' know if we'll make it.

FIRST READ

1. The man took off his dark, stained hat and stood with a curious **humility** in front of the screen. "Could you see your way to sell us a loaf of bread, ma'am?"

2. Mae said, "This ain't a grocery store. We got bread to make san'widges."

3. "I know, ma'am." His humility was **insistent**. "We need bread and there ain't nothin' for quite a piece, they say."

4. "'F we sell bread we gonna run out." Mae's tone was faltering.

5. "We're hungry," the man said.

6. "Whyn't you buy a san'widge? We got nice san'widges, hamburgs."

7. "We'd sure admire to do that, ma'am. But we can't. We got to make a dime do all of us." And he said embarrassedly, "We ain't got but a little."

8. Mae said, "You can't get no loaf a bread for a dime. We only got fifteen-cent loafs."

9. From behind her Al growled, "God Almighty, Mae, give 'em bread."

10. "We'll run out 'fore the bread truck comes."

11. "Run out then, goddamn it," said Al. He looked sullenly down at the potato salad he was mixing.

12. Mae shrugged her plump shoulders and looked to the truck drivers to show them what she was up against.

13. She held the screen door open and the man came in, bringing a smell of sweat with him. The boys edged behind him and they went immediately to

Please note that excerpts and passages in the StudySync® library and this workbook are intended as touchstones to generate interest in an author's work. The excerpts and passages do not substitute for the reading of entire texts, and StudySync® strongly recommends that students seek out and purchase the whole literary or informational work in order to experience it as the author intended. Links to online resellers are available in our digital library. In addition, complete works may be ordered through an authorized reseller by filling out and returning to StudySync® the order form enclosed in this workbook.

Reading & Writing Companion   **51**

NOTES

the candy case and stared in—not with craving or with hope or even with desire, but just with a kind of wonder that such things could be. They were alike in size and their faces were alike. One scratched his dusty ankle with the toe nails of his other foot. The other whispered some soft message and then they straightened their arms so that their clenched fists in the overall pockets showed through the thin blue cloth.

14 Mae opened a drawer and took out a long waxpaper-wrapped loaf. "This here is a fifteen-cent loaf."

15 The man put his hat back on his head. He answered with **inflexible** humility, "Won't you—can't you see your way to cut off ten cents' worth?"

16 Al said snarlingly, "Goddamn it, Mae. Give 'em the loaf."

17 The man turned toward Al. "No, we want ta buy ten cents' worth of it. We got it figgered awful close, mister, to get to California."

18 Mae said **resignedly**, "You can have this for ten cents."

19 "That'd be robbin' you, ma'am."

20 "Go ahead—Al says to take it." She pushed the waxpapered loaf across the counter. The man took a deep leather pouch from his rear pocket, untied the strings, and spread it open. It was heavy with silver and with greasy bills.

21 "May soun' funny to be so tight," he apologized. "We got a thousan' miles to go, an' we don' know if we'll make it."

22 He dug in the pouch with a forefinger, located a dime, and pinched in for it. When he put it down on the counter he had a penny with it. He was about to drop the penny back into the pouch when his eye fell on the boys frozen before the candy counter. He moved slowly down to them. He pointed in the case at big long sticks of striped peppermint.

23 "Is them penny candy, ma'am?"

24 Mae moved down and looked in. "Which ones?"

25 "There, them stripy ones."

26 The little boys raised their eyes to her face and they stopped breathing; their mouths were partly opened, their halfnaked bodies were rigid.

27 "Oh—them. Well, no—them's two for a penny."

28 "Well, gimme two then, ma'am." He placed the copper cent carefully on the counter. The boys **expelled** their held breath softly. Mae held the big sticks out.

Excerpted from *The Grapes of Wrath* by John Steinbeck, published by the Penguin Group.

THINK QUESTIONS   CA-CCSS: CA.RL.9-10.1, CA.L.9-10.4a, CA.L.9-10.4c, CA.L.9-10.4d

1. Why does the man not use more money from his pouch to get more food that the family wants or needs? Use textual evidence to support your answer.

2. What does the children's reaction to seeing the candy say about their experiences in life so far? How does this moment elicit the reader's empathy? Explain your answer with textual evidence.

3. The dialogue of the characters is written to show their dialect, or the particular way they pronounce words and use language based on where they are from and other factors. How does the use of dialogue help the reader to better understand the characters? Cite textual evidence from the passage to support your answer.

4. Use context to determine the meaning of the word **resignedly** as it is used in *The Grapes of Wrath* excerpt. Write your definition of "resignedly" here and explain how you used context to determine the meaning. Then check your inferred meaning in a print or digital dictionary.

5. Considering that the prefix *in-* means "not," and the Latin root *flex* means "bend," what do you think **inflexible** means in this passage? Use context clues to help you determine the meaning. Write your definition of "inflexible" here, and explain how you verified your preliminary determination of the meaning.

Please note that excerpts and passages in the StudySync® library and this workbook are intended as touchstones to generate interest in an author's work. The excerpts and passages do not substitute for the reading of entire texts, and StudySync® strongly recommends that students seek out and purchase the whole literary or informational work in order to experience it as the author intended. Links to online resellers are available in our digital library. In addition, complete works may be ordered through an authorized reseller by filling out and returning to StudySync® the order form enclosed in this workbook.

Reading & Writing Companion

53

CLOSE READ
CA-CCSS: CA.RL.9-10.1, CA.RL.9-10.2, CA.RL.9-10.3, CA.RL.9-10.7, CA.W.9-10.4, CA.W.9-10.5, CA.W.9-10.6, CA.W.9-10.9a, CA.W.9-10.10

Reread the excerpt from *The Grapes of Wrath*. As you reread, complete the Focus Questions below. Then use your answers and annotations from the questions to help you complete the Writing Prompt.

 FOCUS QUESTIONS

1. As you reread the excerpt from *The Grapes of Wrath,* highlight descriptions and dialogue that make the characters and setting seem realistic. Who are the people who visit the diner, and how are they similar to and different from the workers there? Use textual evidence to support your ideas.

2. Think about the other texts you have read in the unit, such as Steinbeck's magazine account of life during the Dust Bowl, *Harvest Gypsies,* and Starr's *Endangered Dreams: The Great Depression in California,* which includes information about one of Dorothea Lange's photographs of the time. What does Steinbeck's novel accomplish that is different from what an article or a photograph can do? Cite textual evidence to help explain your views.

3. What does the dialogue spoken by Al and Mae reveal about their characters? Do you think Mae changes as a result of this encounter with the man and his children? Highlight details and cite textual evidence to support your inference.

4. What theme is Steinbeck developing in this excerpt? Summarize the excerpt and explain, using textual evidence, what this small scene reveals about the behavior of some people during difficult times.

5. Think about the empathy you feel for the characters in this excerpt. How is this different from the empathy you feel for the people in some of the photographs you've seen of the Dust Bowl years? Describe the feeling you get when you see the photograph of the person sitting next to a car on a dirt road (at the 00:09 mark in the Intro video to this lesson).

WRITING PROMPT

Imagine you are a critic writing about the important works of art from the Great Depression. Examine the excerpt from *The Grapes of Wrath* and one of the photographs below. Write a brief informative/explanatory essay that analyzes how the photograph adds to the reader's understanding of the content of the printed text. Include a topic sentence, or thesis statement, and develop it with well-chosen, relevant, and sufficient facts and concrete details from each medium. Be sure to include a description of the photograph you chose to aid readers' comprehension.

TUESDAY SIESTA

FICTION
Gabriel García Márquez
1962

INTRODUCTION

G abriel García Márquez was a Colombian writer who earned international fame popularizing a literary style called magical realism. His most widely read work, the novel *One Hundred Years of Solitude*, has been translated into dozens of languages and has sold millions of copies worldwide. In 1982, García Márquez received the highest international award for writing—the Nobel Prize in Literature. Here, in "Tuesday Siesta," he tells the story a mother and daughter who ride a train to a distant village to visit the grave of a relative.

"'It's an emergency,' the woman insisted. Her voice showed a calm determination."

 FIRST READ

1 The train emerged from the quivering tunnel of sandy rocks, began to cross the symmetrical, interminable banana plantations, and the air became humid and they couldn't feel the sea breeze any more. A stifling blast of smoke came in the car window. On the narrow road parallel to the railway there were oxcarts loaded with green bunches of bananas. Beyond the road, in uncultivated spaces set at odd intervals there were offices with electric fans, red-brick buildings, and residences with chairs and little white tables on the terraces among dusty palm trees and rose-bushes. It was eleven in the morning, and the heat had not yet begun.

2 "You'd better close the window," the woman said. "Your hair will get full of soot." The girl tried to, but the shade wouldn't move because of the rust.

3 They were the only passengers in the lone third-class car. Since the smoke of the locomotive kept coming through the window, the girl left her seat and put down the only things they had with them: a plastic sack with some things to eat and a bouquet of flowers wrapped in newspaper. She sat on the opposite seat, away from the window, facing her mother. They were both in severe and poor mourning clothes.

4 The girl was twelve years old, and it was the first time she'd ever been on a train. The woman seemed too old to be her mother, because of the blue veins on her eyelids and her small, soft, and shapeless body, in a dress cut like a cassock. She was riding with her spinal column braced firmly against the back of the seat, and held a peeling patent-leather handbag in her lap with both hands. She bore the conscientious serenity of someone accustomed to poverty.

5 By twelve the heat had begun. The train stopped for ten minutes to take on water at a station where there was no town. Outside, in the mysterious silence

of the plantations, the shadows seemed clean. But the still air inside the car smelled like untanned leather. The train did not pick up speed. It stopped at two identical towns with wooden houses painted bright colors. The woman's head nodded and she sank into sleep. The girl took off her shoes. Then she went to the washroom to put the bouquet of flowers in some water.

6 When she came back to her seat, her mother was waiting to eat. She gave her a piece of cheese, half a cornmeal pancake, and a cookie, and took an equal portion out of the plastic sack for herself. While they ate, the train crossed an iron bridge very slowly and passed a town just like the ones before, except that in this one there was a crowd in the plaza. A band was playing a lively tune under the oppressive sun. At the other side of town the plantations ended in a plain which was cracked from the drought.

7 The woman stopped eating.

8 "Put on your shoes," she said.

9 The girl looked outside. She saw nothing but the **deserted** plain, where the train began to pick up speed again, but she put the last piece of cookie into the sack and quickly put on her shoes. The woman gave her a comb.

10 "Comb your hair," she said.

11 The train whistle began to blow while the girl was combing her hair. The woman dried the sweat from her neck and wiped the oil from her face with her fingers. When the girl stopped combing, the train was passing the outlying houses of a town larger but sadder than the earlier ones.

12 "If you feel like doing anything, do it now," said the woman. "Later, don't take a drink anywhere even if you're dying of thirst. Above all, no crying."

13 The girl nodded her head. A dry, burning wind came in the window, together with the locomotive's whistle and the clatter of the old cars. The woman folded the plastic bag with the rest of the food and put it in the handbag.

14 For a moment a complete picture of the town, on that bright August Tuesday, shone in the window. The girl wrapped the flowers in the soaking-wet newspapers, moved a little farther away from the window, and stared at her mother. She received a pleasant expression in return. The train began to whistle and slowed down. A moment later it stopped.

15 There was no one at the station. On the other side of the street, on the sidewalk shaded by the almond trees, only the pool hall was open. The town was floating in the heat. The woman and the girl got off the train and crossed

Please note that excerpts and passages in the StudySync® library and this workbook are intended as touchstones to generate interest in an author's work. The excerpts and passages do not substitute for the reading of entire texts, and StudySync® strongly recommends that students seek out and purchase the whole literary or informational work in order to experience it as the author intended. Links to online resellers are available in our digital library. In addition, complete works may be ordered through an authorized reseller by filling out and returning to StudySync® the order form enclosed in this workbook.

Reading & Writing Companion   57

the abandoned station—the tiles split apart by the grass growing up between—and over to the shady side of the street.

16   It was almost two. At that hour, weighted down by drowsiness, the town was taking a **siesta**. The stores, the town offices, the public school were closed at eleven, and didn't reopen until a little before four, when the train went back. Only the hotel across from the station, with its bar and pool hall, and the telegraph office at one side of the plaza stayed open. The houses, most of them built on the banana company's model, had their doors locked from inside and their blinds drawn. In some of them it was so hot that the residents ate lunch in the patio. Others leaned a chair against the wall, in the shade of the almond trees, and took their siesta right out in the street.

17   Keeping to the protective shade of the almond trees, the woman and the girl entered the town without disturbing the siesta. They went directly to the parish house. The woman scratched the metal grating on the door with her fingernail, waited a moment, and scratched again. An electric fan was humming inside. They did not hear the steps. They hardly heard the slight creaking of a door, and immediately a cautious voice, right next to the metal grating: "Who is it?" The woman tried to see through the grating.

18   "I need the priest," she said.

19   "He's sleeping now."

20   "It's an emergency," the woman insisted. Her voice showed a calm determination.

21   The door was opened a little way, noiselessly, and a plump, older woman appeared, with very pale skin and hair the color of iron. Her eyes seemed too small behind her thick eyeglasses.

22   "Come in," she said, and opened the door all the way.

23   They entered a room permeated with an old smell of flowers. The woman of the house led them to a wooden bench and signaled them to sit down. The girl did so, but her mother remained standing, absentmindedly, with both hands clutching the handbag. No noise could be heard above the electric fan.

24   The woman of the house reappeared at the door at the far end of the room. "He says you should come back after three," she said in a very low voice. "He just lay down five minutes ago."

25   "The train leaves at three thirty," said the woman.

26   It was a brief and self-assured reply, but her voice remained pleasant, full of undertones. The woman of the house smiled for the first time.

27   "All right," she said.

28   When the far door closed again, the woman sat down next to her daughter. The narrow waiting room was poor, neat, and clean. On the other side of the wooden railing which divided the room, there was a worktable, a plain one with an oilcloth cover, and on top of the table a primitive typewriter next to a vase of flowers. The parish records were beyond. You could see that it was an office kept in order by a **spinster**.

29   The far door opened and this time the priest appeared, cleaning his glasses with a handkerchief. Only when he put them on was it evident that he was the brother of the woman who had opened the door.

30   "How can I help you?" he asked.

31   "The keys to the cemetery," said the woman.

32   The girl was seated with the flowers in her lap and her feet crossed under the bench. The priest looked at her, then looked at the woman, and then through the wire mesh of the window at the bright, cloudless sky.

33   "In this heat," he said. "You could have waited until the sun went down."

34   The woman moved her head silently. The priest crossed to the other side of the railing, took out of the cabinet a notebook covered in oilcloth, a wooden penholder, and an inkwell, and sat down at the table. There was more than enough hair on his hands to account for what was missing on his head.

35   "Which grave are you going to visit?" he asked.

36   "Carlos Centeno's," said the woman.

37   "Who?"

38   "Carlos Centeno," the woman repeated.

39   The priest still did not understand.

40   "He's the thief who was killed here last week," said the woman in the same tone of voice. "I am his mother."

41   The priest **scrutinized** her. She stared at him with quiet self-control, and the Father blushed. He lowered his head and began to write. As he filled the page, he asked the woman to identify herself, and she replied unhesitatingly,

with precise details, as if she were reading them. The Father began to sweat. The girl unhooked the buckle of her left shoe, slipped her heel out of it, and rested it on the bench rail. She did the same with the right one.

42 It had all started the Monday of the previous week, at three in the morning, a few blocks from there. Rebecca, a lonely widow who lived in a house full of odds and ends, heard above the sound of the drizzling rain someone trying to force the front door from outside. She got up, rummaged around in her closet for an ancient revolver that no one had fired since the days of Colonel Aureliano Buendia, and went into the living room without turning on the lights. Orienting herself not so much by the noise at the lock as by a terror developed in her by twenty eight years of loneliness, she fixed in her imagination not only the spot where the door was but also the exact height of the lock. She clutched the weapon with both hands, closed her eyes, and squeezed the trigger. It was the first time in her life that she had fired a gun. Immediately after the explosion, she could hear nothing except the murmur of the drizzle on the galvanized roof. Then she heard a little metallic bump on the cement porch, and a very low voice, pleasant but terribly exhausted: "Ah, Mother." The man they found dead in front of the house in the morning, his nose blown to bits, wore a flannel shirt with colored stripes, everyday pants with a rope for a belt, and was barefoot. No one in town knew him.

43 "So his name was Carlos Centeno," murmured the Father when he finished writing.

44 "Centeno Ayala," said the woman. "He was my only boy."

45 The priest went back to the cabinet. Two big rusty keys hung on the inside of the door; the girl imagined, as her mother had when she was a girl and as the priest himself must have imagined at some time, that they were Saint Peter's keys. He took them down, put them on the open notebook on the railing, and pointed with his forefinger to a place on the page he had just written, looking at the woman.

46 "Sign here."

47 The woman scribbled her name, holding the handbag under her arm. The girl picked up the flowers, came to the railing shuffling her feet, and watched her mother attentively.

48 The priest sighed.

49 "Didn't you ever try to get him on the right track?"

50 The woman answered when she finished signing.

51   "He was a very good man."

52   The priest looked first at the woman and then at the girl, and realized with a kind of pious amazement that they were not about to cry. The woman continued in the same tone:

53   "I told him never to steal anything that anyone needed to eat, and he minded me. On the other hand, before, when he used to box, he used to spend three days in bed, exhausted from being punched."

54   "All his teeth had to be pulled out," interrupted the girl.

55   "That's right," the woman agreed. "Every mouthful I ate those days tasted of the beatings my son got on Saturday nights."

56   "God's will is **inscrutable**," said the Father.

57   But he said it without much conviction, partly because experience had made him a little skeptical and partly because of the heat. He suggested that they cover their heads to guard against sunstroke. Yawning, and now almost completely asleep, he gave them instructions about how to find Carlos Centeno's grave. When they came back, they didn't have to knock. They should put the key under the door; and in the same place, if they could, they should put an offering for the Church. The woman listened to his directions with great attention, but thanked him without smiling.

58   The Father had noticed that there was someone looking inside, his nose pressed against the metal grating, even before he opened the door to the street. Outside was a group of children. When the door was opened wide, the children scattered. Ordinarily, at that hour there was no one in the street. Now there were not only children. There were groups of people under the almond trees. The Father scanned the street swimming in the heat and then he understood. Softly, he closed the door again.

59   "Wait a moment," he said without looking at the woman.

60   His sister appeared at the far door with a black jacket over her nightshirt and her hair down over her shoulders. She looked silently at the Father.

61   "What was it?" he asked.

62   "The people have noticed," murmured his sister.

63   "You'd better go out by the door to the patio," said the Father.

64   "It's the same there," said his sister. "Everybody is at the windows."

65 The woman seemed not to have understood until then. She tried to look into the street through the metal grating. Then she took the bouquet of flowers from the girl and began to move toward the door. The girl followed her.

66 "Wait until the sun goes down," said the Father.

67 "You'll melt," said his sister, motionless at the back of the room. "Wait and I'll lend you a parasol."

68 "Thank you," replied the woman. "We're all right this way."

69 She took the girl by the hand and went into the street.

Gabriel García Márquez. "La siesta del martes," LOS FUNERALES DE LA MAMÁ GRANDE © Gabriel García Márquez, 1962 y Herederos de Gabriel García Márquez.

THINK QUESTIONS   CA-CCSS: CA.RL.9-10.1, CA.L.9-10.4a, CA.L.9-10.4b, CA.L.9-10.4c, CA.L.9-10.4d

1. Identify details from paragraphs 1–3 to explain to what social class the mother and daughter belong. Why might the author want us to know about their social class?

2. What is the mother like in this story? Cite textual details to show how the author (or narrator) reveals the character of the mother, and justify your inferences.

3. The author chooses not to explain what has happened to the woman's son until paragraph 42, which is past the halfway point in the story. What hints does the author provide as to why the mother and daughter have come to this town? Cite textual evidence and explain your inferences.

4. Use context as a clue to determine the meaning of the word **spinster** as it is used in paragraph 28 of "Tuesday Siesta." Write your definition of "spinster." Then verify your inferred meaning of the word in context or in a print or digital dictionary.

5. The words **inscrutable, scrutiny,** and **scrutinize** have the same root, from the Latin *scrutari,* meaning "to examine or search." What part of speech is **scrutinized,** as it is used in paragraph 41 of "Tuesday Siesta"? Consult general or specialized reference materials, such as a print or digital dictionary, to clarify the word's part of speech.

CLOSE READ
CA-CCSS: CA.RL.9-10.1, CA.RL.9-10.2, CA.RL.9-10.3, CA.RL.9-10.5, CA.RL.9-10.6, CA.W.9-10.4, CA.W.9-10.5, CA.W.9-10.6, CA.W.9-10.9b. CA.W.9-10.10

Reread the excerpt from *Tuesday Siesta*. As you reread, complete the Focus Questions below. Then use your answers and annotations from the questions to help you complete the Writing Prompt.

FOCUS QUESTIONS

1. As you reread the beginning of "Tuesday Siesta," think about how the author structures paragraphs 1–4 by describing the characters and the setting. Think about what the author includes, and what he leaves out. What effect does the author achieve? Highlight textual evidence and use the annotation tool to explain each of your choices. Then summarize your annotations in two or three sentences.

2. The mother makes certain demands on her daughter in paragraphs 2, 8, 10, and 12. What demands does she make? Why does she make them? How might they also represent the larger cultural context of the selection? Highlight textual evidence to support your ideas and write annotations to explain your choices.

3. Religion is part of the cultural context of the story. What is the role of the priest in the town? How does the priest function in the story's plot structure? Highlight evidence, including what the priest says and does, as well as how the mother interacts with him. Support your inferences with specific textual evidence.

4. The author reveals in a flashback something that happened to the woman's son. Describe what happened. Why do you think García Márquez chose to use a flashback? What effect does it have on your understanding of all the events of the plot that have come before? Highlight your evidence from the text and make annotations to explain the effect.

5. Do you think the author wants the reader to feel empathy for the main characters? Why or why not? Do any of the other characters empathize with them? How might the compassion felt by the reader help you to better understand the theme (or message) of the text? Use details and evidence from the text to support your responses.

WRITING PROMPT

Think about the way that Gabriel García Márquez chose to structure the text of "Tuesday Siesta." Consider how he developed the plot by presenting a sequence of events, manipulating time with a flashback, and creating effects such as drama, tension, and surprise. Now it's your turn to structure a text. Write a personal narrative about an event in your life when you met someone from another culture and learned something surprising or interesting about that culture. What was the situation? Who was involved? What was the setting or background? Remember that your personal narrative should be told from the *I* or *we* point of view since you are telling about a true event from your life. Be sure to include a strong introduction, and sequence your events in time order. Include dialogue and descriptive details. Tell what you learned from this cultural experience and how you could apply it to your life. What message about culture would you like to leave with your readers?

LIVING TO TELL THE TALE

NON-FICTION
Gabriel García Márquez
2003

INTRODUCTION

In this excerpt from his autobiography, Gabriel García Márquez recounts the real-life events that inspired him to write "Tuesday Siesta." On a trip back to his hometown, which is poor and in disrepair, García Márquez is reminded of an incident years ago in which a thief was shot and killed trying to break into a house—an event that left a profound and lasting impact on the author.

"Everything was identical to my memories, but smaller and poorer, and leveled by a windstorm of fatality."

 FIRST READ

 NOTES

Excerpt from Chapter 1

1   While the train stood there I had the sensation that we were not altogether alone. But when it pulled away, with an immediate, heart-wrenching blast of its whistle, my mother and I were left forsaken beneath the infernal sun, and all the heavy grief of the town came down on us. But we did not say anything to each other. The old wooden station with its tin roof and running balcony was like a tropical version of the ones we knew from westerns. We crossed the deserted station whose tiles were beginning to crack under the pressure of grass, and we sank into the **torpor** of siesta as we sought the protection of the almond trees.

2   Since I was a boy I had despised those **inert** siestas because we did not know what to do. "Be quiet, we're sleeping," the sleepers would murmur without waking. Stores, public offices, and schools closed at twelve and did not open again until a little before three. The interiors of the houses floated in a limbo of lethargy. In some it was so unbearable that people would hang their hammocks in the courtyard or place chairs in the shade of the almond trees and sleep sitting up in the middle of the street. Only the hotel across from the station, with its bar and billiard room, and the telegraph office behind the church remained open. Everything was identical to my memories, but smaller and poorer, and leveled by a windstorm of fatality: the decaying houses themselves, the tin roofs perforated by rust, the levee with its crumbling granite benches and **melancholy** almond trees, and all of it transfigured by the invisible burning dust that deceived the eye and calcinated the skin. On the other side of the train tracks the private paradise of the banana company, stripped now of its electrified wire fence, was a vast thicket with no palm trees, ruined houses among the poppies, and the rubble of the hospital destroyed by fire. There was not a single door, a crack in a wall, a human trace that did not find a supernatural resonance in me.

3   My mother held herself very erect as she walked with her light step, almost not perspiring in her funereal dress, and in absolute silence, but her mortal pallor and sharpened profile revealed what was happening to her on the inside.

4   When we turned the corner, the dust burned my feet through the weave of my sandals. The feeling of being forsaken became unbearable. Then I saw myself and I saw my mother, just as I saw, when I was a boy, the mother and sister of the thief whom Maria Consuegra had killed with a single shot one week earlier, when he tried to break into her house.

5   At three in the morning the sound of someone trying to force the street door from the outside had wakened her. She got up without lighting the lamp, felt around in the armoire for an archaic revolver that no one had fired since the War of a Thousand Days, and located in the darkness not only the place where the door was but also the exact height of the lock. Then she aimed the weapon with both hands, closed her eyes, and squeezed the trigger. She had never fired a gun before, but the shot hit its target through the door.

6   He was the first dead person I had seen. When I passed by at seven in the morning on my way to school, the body was still lying on the sidewalk in a patch of dried blood, the face destroyed by the lead that had shattered its nose and come out one ear. He was wearing a sailor's T-shirt with colored stripes and ordinary trousers held up by a rope instead of a belt, and he was barefoot. At his side, on the ground, they found the homemade picklock with which he had tried to jimmy the lock.

7   The town dignitaries came to Maria Consuegra's house to offer her their condolences for having killed the thief. I went that night with Papalelo, and we found her sitting in an armchair from Manila that looked like an enormous wicker peacock, surrounded by the fervor of her friends who listened to the story she had repeated a thousand times. Everyone agreed with her that she had fired out of sheer fright. It was then that my grandfather asked her if she had heard anything after the shot, and she answered that the first she had heard a great silence, then the metallic sound of the picklock falling on the cement, and then a faint, anguished voice: "Mother, help me!" Maria Consuegra, it seemed, had not been conscious of this heart-breaking **lament** until my grandfather asked her the question. Only then did she burst into tears.

8   This happened on a Monday. On Tuesday of the following week, during siesta, I was playing tops with Luis Carmelo Correa, my oldest friend in life, when we were surprised by the sleepers waking before it was time and looking out the windows. Then we saw in the deserted street a woman dressed in strict mourning and a girl about twelve years old who was carrying

NOTES

a bouquet of faded flowers wrapped in newspaper. They protected themselves from the burning sun with a black umbrella and were quite oblivious to the **effrontery** of the people who watched them pass by. They were the mother and younger sister of the dead thief, bringing flowers for his grave.

9   That vision pursued me for many years, like a single dream that the entire town watched through its windows as it passed, until I managed to exorcise it in a story. But the truth is that I did not become aware of the drama of the woman and the girl, or their **imperturbable** dignity, until the day I went with my mother to sell the house and surprised myself walking down the same deserted street at the same lethal hour.

10   "I feel as if I were the thief," I said.

11   My mother did not understand me. In fact, when we passed the house of Maria Consuegra she did not even glance at the door where you could still see the patched bullet hole in the wood. Years later, recalling that trip with her, I confirmed that she did remember the tragedy but would have given her soul to forget it.

Excerpted from *Living to Tell the Tale* by Gabriel García Márquez, published by Vintage Books.

 THINK QUESTIONS   CA-CCSS: CA.RI.9-10.1, CA.L.9-10.4a, CA.L.9-10.4d, CA.L.9-10.5a

1.   This excerpt, from the autobiography of Gabriel García Márquez, explores a boyhood memory that "pursued" him "for many years." Highlight details from the text that signal to the reader that the author is recalling a vivid memory. How is this writing similar to fiction? Cite textual evidence to explain how the tradition of the siesta connects to memories that the author discusses in the excerpt.

2.   The author describes an incident that affected him deeply as a child. What happened and why did it affect him so strongly? Refer to several details from the text to support your answer.

3.   Why did Maria Consuegra burst into tears when she spoke to the author's grandfather? Cite specific evidence from paragraph 7 to support your answer.

4.   Use context to determine the meaning of the word **torpor** as it is used in the first paragraph of "Living to Tell the Tale." Write your definition of "torpor," and verify your inferred meaning of the word in a print or digital dictionary.

5.   In the second paragraph, García Márquez uses the phrase "melancholy almond trees" in describing his town. What clues from the text help you determine the meaning of **melancholy**? Write your definition of "melancholy" and verify your meaning by checking it in context.

CLOSE READ

CA-CCSS: CA.RI.9-10.1, CA.RI.9-10.2, CA.RI.9-10.3, CA.RI.9-10.6, CA.RI.9-10.7, CA.W.9-10.4, CA.W.9-10.5, CA.W.9-10.6, CA.W.9-10.9b, CA.W.9-10.10

Reread the excerpt from *Living to Tell the Tale*. As you reread, complete the Focus Questions below. Then use your answers and annotations from the questions to help you complete the Writing Prompt.

 FOCUS QUESTIONS

1. As you reread the beginning of this excerpt from the autobiography *Living to Tell the Tale,* compare and contrast it with how Gabriel García Márquez begins his short story "Tuesday Siesta." How are the details similar in each version of events? How are they different? What does the author emphasize in each version? Highlight textual evidence to support your ideas and write annotations to explain your choices.

2. How does García Márquez develop the events in his autobiography? What overall shape does he give the text structure by unfolding events in a certain order? Highlight events (or episodes) that stand out for you. Cite specific evidence from the text, and annotate to explain your choices.

3. In the third paragraph of *Living to Tell the Tale,* García Márquez describes his mother. How does the image of her connect to the events he describes? Compare the description of his mother with that of the mother in "Tuesday

Siesta." What evidence in the two texts supports the central idea or theme of the mothers as women who maintain their dignity under tragic circumstances. Draw inferences from the text, and highlight specific textual evidence to support your analysis.

4. What is the central (or main) idea of this excerpt from *Living to Tell the Tale*? Restate the central idea of the text in one or two sentences, and support your response with specific details from the text.

5. In paragraph 10, García Márquez says to his mother, "'I feel as if I were the thief.'" What makes him feel empathy for the thief? Who else does he empathize with? How might his empathy (sharing of another's feelings) suggest his purpose for writing about this event? Annotate to explain your ideas. Highlight specific evidence from the text to support your explanation.

WRITING PROMPT

The episode that Gabriel García Márquez recounts in his short story, "Tuesday Siesta," is based on real events that he wrote in his autobiography, *Living to Tell the Tale*. How does the author transform a boyhood memory into a short story? Write a response in which you compare and contrast this excerpt from his autobiography with the story "Tuesday Siesta." In your response, analyze what is emphasized or absent in each account. Finally, compare and contrast the order of events presented in the autobiography with the order of events presented in the plot structure of the short story. Support your analysis with strong textual evidence.

Copyright © BookheadEd Learning, LLC

THE ELEPHANT MAN

DRAMA
Bernard Pomerance
1979

INTRODUCTION

Bernard Pomerance's award-winning play was based on the life of Joseph (also known as John) Merrick, a Victorian-era British man born with a bone disease that caused his limbs and skull to become grossly oversized. His condition made him a freak show attraction and a witty favorite of the aristocracy, but he never realized his dream of feeling normal.

"The deformities rendered the face utterly incapable of the expression of any emotion..."

 FIRST READ

SCENE II: ART IS AS NOTHING TO NATURE

1 *[Whitechapel Rd. A storefront. A large advertisement of a creature with an elephant's head. ROSS, his manager.]*

2 ROSS: **Tuppence** only, step in and see: This side of the grave, John Merrick has no hope nor expectation of relief. In every sense his situation is desperate. His physical agony is exceeded only by his mental anguish, a despised creature without consolation. Tuppence only, step in and see! To live with his physical hideousness, incapacitating deformities and **unremitting** pain is trial enough, but to be exposed to the cruelly lacerating expressions of horror and disgust by all who behold him—is even more difficult to bear. Tuppence only, step in and see! For in order to survive, Merrick forces himself to suffer these humiliations, in order to survive, thus he exposes himself to crowds who pay to gape and **yawp** at this freak of nature, the Elephant Man.

3 *[Enter TREVES who looks at advertisement.]*

4 ROSS: See Mother Nature uncorseted and in **malignant** rage! Tuppence.

5 TREVES: The sign's absurd. Half-elephant, half-man is not possible. Is he foreign?

6 ROSS: Right, from Leicester. But nothing to fear.

7 TREVES: I'm at the London across the road. I would be curious to see him if there is more genuine disorder. If he is a mass of papier-mâché and paint however—

8 ROSS: Then pay me nothing. Enter sir. Merrick, stand up. Ya bloody donkey, up, up.

9   *[They go in, then emerge. TREVES pays.]*

10   TREVES: I must examine him further at the hospital. Here is my card. I'm Treves. I will have a cab pick him up and return him. My card will gain him admittance.

11   ROSS: Five bob he's yours for the day.

12   TREVES: I wish to examine him in the interests of science, you see.

13   ROSS: Sir, I'm Ross. I look out for him, get him his living. Found him in Leicester workhouse. His own ma put him there age of three. Couldn't bear the sight, well you can see why. We—he and I—are in business. He is our capital, see. Go to a bank. Go anywhere. Want to borrow capital, you pay interest. Scientists even. He's good value though. You won't find another like him.

14   TREVES: Fair enough. *[He pays.]*

15   ROSS: Right. Out here, Merrick. Ya bloody donkey, out!

16   *[Lights fade out.]*

SCENE III: WHO HAS SEEN THE LIKE OF THIS?

17   [TREVES *lectures.* MERRICK *contorts himself to approximate projected slides of the real Merrick.*]

18   TREVES: The most striking feature about him was his enormous head. Its circumference was about that of a man's waist. From the brow there projected a huge bony mass like a loaf, while from the back of his head hung a bag of spongy fungous-looking skin, the surface of which was comparable to brown cauliflower. On the top of the skull were a few long lank hairs. The **osseous** growth on the forehead, at this stage about the size of a tangerine, almost occluded one eye. From the upper jaw there projected another mass of bone. It protruded from the mouth like a pink stump, turning the upper lip inside out, and making the mouth a wide slobbering aperture. The nose was merely a lump of flesh, only recognizable as a nose from its position. The deformities rendered the face utterly incapable of the expression of any emotion whatsoever. The back was horrible because from it hung, as far down as the middle of the thigh, huge sacklike masses of flesh covered by the same loathsome cauliflower stain. The right arm was of enormous size and shapeless. It suggested but was not elephantiasis, and was overgrown also with pendant masses of the same cauliflower-like skin. The right hand was large and clumsy—a fin or paddle rather than a hand. No distinction existed between the palm and back, the thumb was like a radish, the fingers like thick **tuberous** roots. As a limb it was useless. The other arm was

NOTES

remarkable by contrast. It was not only normal but was moreover a delicately shaped limb covered with a fine skin and provided with a beautiful hand which any woman might have envied. From the chest hung a bag of the same repulsive flesh. It was like a dewlap suspended from the neck of a lizard. The lower limbs had the characters of the deformed arm. They were unwieldy, dropsical-looking, and grossly misshapen. There arose from the fungous skin growths a very sickening stench which was hard to tolerate. To add a further burden to his trouble, the wretched man when a boy developed hip disease which left him permanently lame, so that he could only walk with a stick. [*to* MERRICK] Please. [MERRICK *walks*.] He was thus denied all means of escape from his tormenters.

19   VOICE: Mr. Treves, you have shown a profound and unknown disorder to us. You have said when he leaves here it is for his exhibition again. I do not think it ought to be permitted. It is a disgrace. It is a pity and a disgrace. It is an indecency in fact. It may be a danger in ways we do not know. Something ought to be done about it.

20   TREVES: I am a doctor. What would you have me do?

21   VOICE: Well. I know what to do. I know.

22   *[Silence. A policeman enters as lights fade out.]*

Excerpted from *The Elephant Man* by Bernard Pomerance, published by Grove Press.

THINK QUESTIONS CA-CCSS: CA.RL.9-10.1, CA.RL.9-10.4, CA.L.9-10.4a, CA.L.9-10.4b

1. To what is Ross beckoning customers? Cite details from the text to explain how you drew your inference.

2. What details provide clues about the time and place in which this play is set? Highlight and annotate to identify the textual evidence that provides clues.

3. Use textual evidence to make an inference about why the author ended the scene (indicated by the stage direction "lights fade out") with the arrival of the police officer.

4. Use context to determine the meaning of the word yawp as it is used in *The Elephant Man*. Write your definition and explain how you arrived at it.

5. Considering that the prefix *mal-* means "bad," what other context clues can you find to help you determine the meaning of the word **malignant** as it is used in the passage? Write your definition of the word "malignant" and explain how you determined it.

CLOSE READ
CA-CCSS: CA.RL.9-10.1, CA.RL.9-10.3, CA.RL.9-10.4, CA.RL.9-10.7, CA.RL.9-10.10, CA.W.9-10.1a, CA.W.9-10.1b, CA.W.9-10.4, CA.W.9-10.5, CA.W.9-10.6, CA.W.9-10.9a, CA.W.9-10.10, CA.L.9-10.5a

Reread the scenes from "The Elephant Man." As you reread, complete the Focus Questions below. Then use your answers and annotations from the questions to help you complete the Writing Prompt.

FOCUS QUESTIONS

1. Reread the second paragraph. How might this help the audience visualize John Merrick? Highlight textual evidence and write an annotation to explain your answer.

2. As you reread the excerpt from *The Elephant Man*, remember that the author communicates the tone through dialogue and stage directions. In the second paragraph, highlight a sentence or phrase that describes how people react when they see Merrick. Then write an annotation to explain how this text contributes to the tone of the play.

3. Think about how the character of "VOICE" (paragraphs 19 and 21) adds a mysterious tone to the play. Highlight the lines that help establish this tone. Then write an annotation giving stage directions that could enhance the mysterious tone of this character. How might this character look, sound, and act?

4. Highlight words or phrases from the first five sentences of paragraph 18 that are examples of the academic and scientific tone of this part of the play. Then make annotations to explain how these words or phrases help create that tone.

5. In their speeches, both Ross and Treves use words and phrases with specific meanings and connotations to describe John Merrick. Highlight some of these words and phrases and explain their meanings and connotations. Then explain how these different descriptions help the audience develop compassion for Merrick. Write your response as an annotation.

WRITING PROMPT

When *The Elephant Man* was performed live on stage, the actor playing John Merrick typically had a natural appearance without elaborate makeup. Instead, the actor would contort his body to portray Merrick's physical challenges. However, in the movie version, the actor was made up to match the descriptions given in the play. Based on the short excerpt you have read, which choice do you think would be more effective in staying true to the author's tone? Write a short response to state your opinion. Support your claim with valid reasons and relevant textual evidence.

Please note that excerpts and passages in the StudySync® library and this workbook are intended as touchstones to generate interest in an author's work. The excerpts and passages do not substitute for the reading of entire texts, and StudySync® strongly recommends that students seek out and purchase the whole literary or informational work in order to experience it as the author intended. Links to online resellers are available in our digital library. In addition, complete works may be ordered through an authorized reseller by filling out and returning to StudySync® the order form enclosed in this workbook.

Reading & Writing Companion

73

MENDING WALL

POETRY
Robert Frost
1914

INTRODUCTION

A four-time winner of the Pulitzer Prize for Poetry, Robert Frost was one of the most popular and critically acclaimed poets the 20th century. Much of his work is set in rural New England, vividly evoking pastoral life in all its trials and beauty. Here, in "Mending Wall," he examines one of the more difficult boundaries to navigate in such a life.

"We keep the wall between us as we go."

FIRST READ

1 Something there is that doesn't love a wall,
2 That sends the frozen-ground-swell under it,
3 And spills the upper boulders in the sun,
4 And makes gaps even two can pass **abreast**.
5 The work of hunters is another thing:
6 I have come after them and made repair
7 Where they have left not one stone on a stone,
8 But they would have the rabbit out of hiding,
9 To please the **yelping** dogs. The gaps I mean,
10 No one has seen them made or heard them made,
11 But at spring **mending**-time we find them there.
12 I let my neighbor know beyond the hill;
13 And on a day we meet to walk the line
14 And set the wall between us once again.
15 We keep the wall between us as we go.
16 To each the boulders that have fallen to each.
17 And some are loaves and some so nearly balls
18 We have to use a spell to make them balance:
19 "Stay where you are until our backs are turned!"
20 We wear our fingers rough with handling them.
21 Oh, just another kind of outdoor game,
22 One on a side. It comes to little more:
23 He is all pine and I am apple-orchard.
24 My apple trees will never get across
25 And eat the cones under his pines, I tell him.
26 He only says, "Good fences make good neighbors."
27 Spring is the mischief in me, and I wonder
28 If I could put a notion in his head:
29 "*Why* do they make good neighbors? Isn't it

Please note that excerpts and passages in the StudySync® library and this workbook are intended as touchstones to generate interest in an author's work. The excerpts and passages do not substitute for the reading of entire texts, and StudySync® strongly recommends that students seek out and purchase the whole literary or informational work in order to experience it as the author intended. Links to online resellers are available in our digital library. In addition, complete works may be ordered through an authorized reseller by filling out and returning to StudySync® the order form enclosed in this workbook.

Reading & Writing
Companion

75

NOTES

30 Where there are cows? But here there are no cows.

31 Before I built a wall I'd ask to know

32 What I was walling in or walling out,

33 And to whom I was like to give **offense**.

34 Something there is that doesn't love a wall,

35 That wants it down!" I could say "Elves" to him,

36 But it's not elves exactly, and I'd rather

37 He said it for himself. I see him there,

38 Bringing a stone grasped firmly by the top

39 In each hand, like an old-stone **savage** armed.

40 He moves in darkness as it seems to me,

41 Not of woods only and the shade of trees.

42 He will not go behind his father's saying,

43 And he likes having thought of it so well

44 He says again, "Good fences make good neighbors."

 THINK QUESTIONS CA-CCSS: CA.RL.9-10.1, CA.L.9-10.4a, CA.L.9-10.4c

1. What task is the author of "Mending Wall" describing in this poem? Why does the job have to be done every year? Highlight and annotate textual evidence to explain your answer.

2. What do you think the neighbor means by the expression, "Good fences make good neighbors"? Find evidence in the poem to explain.

3. What lines from the poem show that the speaker does not completely believe that this task needs to be done every year? How can you tell that the speaker disagrees with his neighbor's statement that "Good fences make good neighbors"? Use textual evidence to explain.

4. Read the lines that include, "To please the yelping dogs." What context clues from the passage help you understand the meaning of **yelping**? What else helps you understand its meaning? Write your definition of "yelping" here and explain how you got it. Then, using a dictionary or similar resource, determine the word's part of speech and precise meaning.

5. Use context to determine the meaning of the word **abreast** as it is used in the poem. Write your definition of "abreast" here and identify the context clues that helped you define it. Then, use a reference work such as a dictionary or thesaurus to determine one or two synonyms for the word and explain how they clarify its meaning.

CLOSE READ

CA-CCSS: CA.RL.9-10.1, CA.RL.9-10.2, CA.RL.9-10.4, CA.W.9-10.1a, CA.W.9-10.1b, CA.W.9-10.4, CA.W.9-10.5, CA.W.9-10.6, CA.W.9-10.9a, CA.W.9-10.10, CA.L.9-10.5a

Reread the poem "Mending Wall." As you reread, complete the Focus Questions below. Then use your answers and annotations from the questions to help you complete the Writing Prompt.

FOCUS QUESTIONS

1. Reread lines 1–5. What do you think is the "something" that "does not love a wall"? How could this be interpreted as a larger idea or theme? Highlight evidence from the text and use the annotation tool to support your answer.

2. Reread lines 17–20 and highlight examples of figurative language being used in these lines. What kinds of figurative language are these, and how do these figures of speech help the reader better understand the actions taking place?

3. Reread lines 26–33. What do you think is meant by the line, "Spring is the mischief in me"? Is this an example of figurative language? If so, what does it compare? Highlight evidence from the text that supports your interpretation.

4. Reread lines 37–41. What can you infer about the speaker's opinion of his neighbor? Support your answer by highlighting evidence from the text and using the annotation tool to explain your interpretation.

5. Do you think that the speaker feels empathy for his neighbor? Why or why not? Use text evidence to support your claim.

WRITING PROMPT

Read the entire poem through again, applying your knowledge of figurative language and textual evidence to interpret each line as you read. Why do you think the speaker of the poem helps to repair the wall every year? How do the poet's descriptions, including figurative language, help express the speaker's feelings about it? If you were in the speaker's position, would you help repair the wall each year? Why or why not? Write a short argumentative essay of 250–300 words in which you take a position on whether the speaker should help repair the wall. Quote textual evidence from the poem, including explanations of metaphors and symbols, to support your ideas.

Please note that excerpts and passages in the StudySync® library and this workbook are intended as touchstones to generate interest in an author's work. The excerpts and passages do not substitute for the reading of entire texts, and StudySync® strongly recommends that students seek out and purchase the whole literary or informational work in order to experience it as the author intended. Links to online resellers are available in our digital library. In addition, complete works may be ordered through an authorized reseller by filling out and returning to StudySync® the order form enclosed in this workbook.

Reading & Writing Companion

77

THE BEST THANKSGIVING EVER

English Language Development

FICTION

INTRODUCTION

Katherine remembers the first Thanksgiving she spent at the "adults" table, instead of at the "kids" table with her cousins. Katherine innocently uncovers a bitter argument and is determined to find the cause. Does she succeed? How will she settle the issue?

"I had no idea what I had done wrong, but I saw that disapproving look in Mom's eye."

FIRST READ

NOTES

1   Cousin Elizabeth always likes to remind me about a Thanksgiving dinner many years ago. It was the day when I got myself into a real bit of trouble. I did not know what I was doing, and I **exposed** a family problem by accident.

2   We celebrated Thanksgiving at my grandparents' apartment. That year was the first time I was old enough to join the "adults'" table. Elizabeth was two years younger and still stuck at the "kids" table. She sure was angry about it. Now that I think about it, Elizabeth being so angry probably accounts for her perfect memory of that challenging day.

3   Thanksgiving dinner was always my favorite **festive** meal, because I got to see family I really liked. I got to eat lots of turkey and sweet potatoes, too. Most of all, I really enjoyed my once-a-year visit with Aunt Alice, Mom's sister. Aunt Alice was a happy woman, always smiling. She always had little gifts hidden in the pockets of her huge, colorful coat, too. "Aunt Alice," I began. "Could I come visit you this summer? I'm old enough to travel alone," I added with more confidence than I felt.

4   "Eat your turkey, Katherine," Mom said quietly.

5   Foolishly, I continued talking. "I could help out in your studio." Aunt Alice was an artist, and she created amazing paintings of plants and flowers.

6   "Katherine! Do not interrupt the adults," Mom snapped. "Will someone pass the cranberry sauce?"

7   I knew Mom had been busy cooking. I think she was tense. I kept talking to fill the silence. Elizabeth always said that had I been more **perceptive,** I would have shut my mouth. "It would be fun!" I insisted.

8   "KATHERINE LILYAN!" Mom warned.

9   Everyone stopped and stared at me. I had no idea what I had done wrong, but I saw that disapproving look in Mom's eye. It was the look that said, "We will have a talk later, young lady. You will be spending time in your room thinking about what you did wrong."

10   Then Grandma joined the **fray.** "I think it would be good for Katherine to spend time with her aunt."

11   Mom began busily slicing the turkey on her plate into tiny little pieces. Aunt Alice **studied** her food like it was a fascinating book.

12   I wanted to know what had happened, but Aunt Alice and Mom ignored me and kept eating. They acted strangely polite, like they had just met and found each other **disagreeable.**

13   Finally, I couldn't take any more of Mom and Aunt Alice's quiet anger. "Why are you two mad at each other?" I blurted out.

14   Aunt Alice gave Mother a challenging look. Then she said, "When Great Aunt Prudence passed on, we were given something that was important to her. She never asked what we wanted. I got her ugly old clock covered in frightening gargoyles. Your MOTHER, however, got Aunt Prudence's vintage turquoise bracelet. The bracelet was beautiful and a reminder of her husband's love."

15   Mom's face hardened. "YOU got a clock," she growled, "that is a handcrafted antique. All I got was that stupid bracelet. Now Katherine, that is the reason Aunt Alice and I do not agree. Your questioning has spoiled Thanksgiving dinner! I hope you are happy!"

16   I sat silently for a minute. It stung to be reprimanded. From the corner of my eye I saw Elizabeth grinning from the kids' table. Then she motioned to the empty seat next to her. I got the point immediately.

17   I kept talking even though I probably should have stopped. "Aunt Alice, you hate the clock, right? But you still keep it, because it came from Great Aunt Prudence. Mom, you keep the bracelet for the same reason. You both have something to remember her by. It seems like that should be more important than who got what."

18   They both stared at me with their mouths hanging open in shock. I quickly picked up my plate, pushed in my seat, and moved back to the kids' table. It seemed like the more mature place to enjoy my holiday.

19   I saw Grandma smother a laugh before standing up and walking toward the kitchen. "Anyone interested in trying my apple pie? Or Alice's pecan pie, or Margaret's pumpkin pie?"

20   Elizabeth and I had a slice of each one.

USING LANGUAGE CA-CCSS: ELD.PII.9-10.2.b.Ex

Complete the chart by writing the matching effect for each cause. Then, write the language clues that signaled the cause and effect relationship in the last column.

Effect Options	Language Clues Options
Thanksgiving is Katherine's favorite meal.	"Then she pointed to the empty seat next to her."
Her cousin suggests Katherine should sit at the kids' table again.	"Now Katherine, that is the reason Aunt Alice and I do not agree."
Her cousin gets mad.	"She sure was angry about it."
Katherine's mom and Aunt Alice are angry at each other.	"Thanksgiving dinner was always my favorite festive meal, because I got to see family I really liked."

Cause	Effect	Language Clues
Katherine is old enough to sit at the adults' table.		
Katherine sees family she really likes at Thanksgiving.		
Aunt Prudence gave Katherine's mom and aunt gifts they did not like.		
Katherine's mother yells at her.		

MEANINGFUL INTERACTIONS CA-CCSS: ELD.PI.9-10.1.Ex, ELD.PI.9-10.6.a.Ex

Work together in small groups to analyze "The Best Thanksgiving Ever" and explain the causes and effects that appear in the plot. Work in small groups to practice sharing and discussing your opinions, using the speaking frames. Then, use the self-assessment rubric to evaluate your participation in the discussion. Remember to focus on the discussion skill of providing coherent and well-articulated comments. Before commenting, ask yourself: *Have I thought through what I want to say? Does what I want to say make sense? Could I express myself any more clearly?*

- One effect of Katherine's curiosity is . . .

- The event that caused the disagreement was . . .

- That event happened because . . .

- One effect of their argument is . . .

- One effect it has on Katherine is . . .

- Another effect on Katherine is . . .

- I think the effect of Katherine's speech at the end will be . . . , because . . .

 SELF-ASSESSMENT RUBRIC CA-CCSS: ELD.PI.9-10.1.Ex,

	4 I did this well.	**3** I did this pretty well.	**2** I did this a little bit.	**1** I did not do this.
I expressed my opinion clearly; my comments were coherent.				
I listened carefully to others' opinions.				
I spoke respectfully when disagreeing with others.				
I was courteous when persuading others to share my view.				

REREAD

Reread paragraphs 1–10 of "The Best Thanksgiving Ever." After you reread, complete the Using Language and Meaningful Interactions activities.

USING LANGUAGE CA-CCSS: ELD.PI.9-10.6.c.Ex

Read each word. Complete the chart by writing the correct meanings from the options below.

Meaning in Text Options	Different Meaning Options
heated argument	different form of a verb
spoke sharply	broke
recollection	records of an amount of money
uptight	unravel

Word	Meaning in Text	Different Meaning
tense		
fray		
accounts		
snapped		

MEANINGFUL INTERACTIONS CA-CCSS: ELD.PI.9-10.1.Ex, ELD.PI.9-10.6.b.Ex

Based on what you have read in "The Best Thanksgiving Ever," what can you infer about Katherine's character? Work with partners in small groups to practice sharing and discussing your opinions, using the speaking frames. Then, use the self-assessment rubric to evaluate your participation in the discussion.

- I think Katherine is . . .

- Some of her actions that support my opinion include . . .

- Other characters describe her as . . .

- As a result, I think that . . .

- Katherine reacts to the situation by . . . , which suggests she . . .

- I think . . . said that . . .

- I agree / don't agree with . . . that . . .

SELF-ASSESSMENT RUBRIC CA-CCSS: ELD.PI.9-10.6.b.Ex

	4 I did this well.	3 I did this pretty well.	2 I did this a little bit.	1 I did not do this.
I expressed my opinion clearly.				
I listened carefully to others' opinions.				
I spoke respectfully when disagreeing with others.				
I was courteous when persuading others to share my view.				
I affirmed others using phrases such as "good idea," "I agree," and "I see your point."				

REREAD

Reread paragraphs 11–20 of "The Best Thanksgiving Ever." After you reread, complete the Using Language and Meaningful Interactions activities.

USING LANGUAGE   CA-CCSS: ELD.PII.9-10.3.Ex

Read each sentence and note the underlined verb. Complete the chart with the correct form of the verb for each tense from the options below.

Options				
spoiled	studied	spoil	talk	talked
will interrupt	will spoil	joined	will study	will join
join	study	will talk	interrupted	interrupt

Sentence in Text	Present Tense	Past Tense	Future Tense
Do not <u>interrupt</u> the adults.			
Then Grandma <u>joined</u> the fray.			
Aunt Alice <u>studied</u> her food like it was a fascinating book.			
You have <u>spoiled</u> Thanksgiving dinner!			
I kept <u>talking</u>.			

MEANINGFUL INTERACTIONS CA-CCSS: ELD.PI.9-10.1.Ex

What do you think about the end of the text? Do you think Margaret and Aunt Alice will reconcile now? Do you think Katherine meant to fix the relationship between her two relatives, or was it an accident? Work with partners or in small groups to practice sharing and discussing your opinions, using the speaking frames.

- In my opinion, Margaret and Aunt Alice . . .

- Words/phrases/dialogue such as . . . suggest that they feel . . .

- I think Katherine did/did not . . . because . . .

- Details such as . . . suggest that Katherine did . . .

- Details that suggest the opposite include . . .

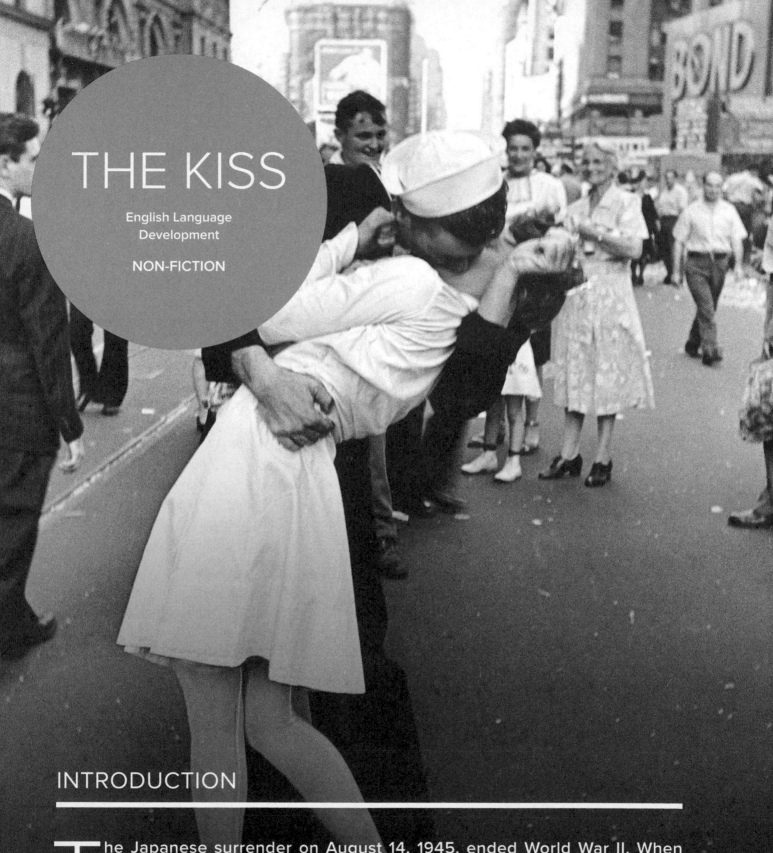

THE KISS

English Language
Development

NON-FICTION

INTRODUCTION

The Japanese surrender on August 14, 1945, ended World War II. When the news spread, people celebrated in the streets. A world famous photographer captured a special moment during the celebration, and the picture became famous. Why did the photo become so famous? And who were

"It became the most famous kiss in American history."

FIRST READ

NOTES

1   During World War II, the United States was involved in two "theaters," or geographical areas—Europe and the Pacific. America joined the Allied forces to end the war in Europe victoriously on V-E Day (Victory in Europe Day), May 8, 1945, but the battles in the Pacific continued. Many people thought that the Japanese would **maintain** their fierce resistance and never surrender to the enemy. However, on August 14, 1945, the Japanese government surrendered to Allied forces. When word reached the United States, cheerful, spontaneous celebrations erupted across the country. The most familiar and remembered celebration occurred in Times Square in New York City. A photograph called "The Kiss" recorded that moment.

2   When news of the Japanese surrender reached New York, people ran into the streets, randomly hugging one another, laughing, singing, and rejoicing. In Times Square, the conventional formal manner of strangers was abandoned. Sailors climbed lampposts to erect American flags. Strings of paper and confetti rained down from windows high above the street. **Elation** spread like giggles in a first-grade classroom.

3   In the midst of this, world-famous photographer Alfred Eisenstaedt began snapping photos of the people expressing their relief and joy. Because of his expertise, he did not need time to set up a memorable picture. Methodical process turned into unplanned work. His purpose was to capture human emotion. One picture, snapped by Eisenstaedt, was that of a sailor kissing a nurse.

4   In the confusion and celebration, Eisenstaedt never got the names and addresses of the couple he photographed. Two weeks later, the photo appeared on the cover of *Life* magazine. It became the most famous kiss in American history. The main idea was to express both love and joy. The photo has become part of American culture to this day. It appears on everything from coffee mugs to calendars. People wanted to know the identity of the

couple, so the search began. In 1979, Eisenstaedt believed he had found the nurse, but the sailor's identity was unknown. But had he actually found the nurse?

5 The mystery continued over the years. The question was always the same: who were these two individuals? Their faces were almost totally hidden in the photo. Many people have claimed to be the couple. Different accounts have commonly appeared in articles and books. Couples, observers, and even a forensic artist confirmed those accounts. Then *The Kissing Sailor,* a book published in 2012, identified the two, who were then in their nineties. The young sailor had **impulsively** grabbed a dental assistant and kissed her. The time, according to them, was about two o'clock.

6 An online discussion, however, suggested the time was around 7:03 p.m., about the time that President Truman announced the surrender of Japan. A person claiming to have witnessed the kiss insists it was around 6 p.m. A physicist and his team then joined the discussion. They carefully studied maps of Times Square made at the time, archival photos, and building blueprints. They believed that observing the shadows cast by the buildings in the picture itself would indicate the **precise** time of the picture. The physicist and his team insisted that the time was actually 5:51 p.m. This, of course, did not identify the pair and might dismiss the claim of the elderly couple mentioned in the book. Nonetheless, the information provided another clue about the photo.

7 By now, many observers and perhaps even the couple themselves have died, but the photograph remains an important part of American culture. In 2005, to celebrate the sixtieth anniversary of V-J Day (Victory over Japan Day), a sculptor created a 25-foot-tall **version** of the familiar kiss. The statue is called *Embracing Peace.* It was placed in Times Square for the 2015 "Kiss-In" event.

USING LANGUAGE CA-CCSS: ELD.PII.9-10.2.a.Ex

Read each sentence. Choose the sentence or phrase that refers to the bolded referring word or phrase.

1. In the midst of **this**, world-famous photographer Alfred Eisenstaedt began snapping photos of the people expressing their relief and joy. (paragraph 3)

   ○ "... the conventional formal manner of strangers was abandoned." (paragraph 2)
   ○ "... people ran into the streets, randomly hugging one another, laughing, singing, and rejoicing." (paragraph 2)

2. In the **confusion and celebration**, Eisenstaedt never got the names and addresses of the couple he photographed. (paragraph 4)

   ○ "... people expressing their relief and joy." (paragraph 3)
   ○ "... he did not need time to set up a memorable picture." (paragraph 3)

3. The **mystery** continued over the years. (paragraph 5)

   ○ "The photo has become part of American culture ..." (paragraph 4)
   ○ "... Eisenstaedt believed he had found the nurse, but the sailor's identity was unknown." (paragraph 4)

4. **This**, of course, did not identify the pair and might dismiss the claim of the elderly couple mentioned in the book. (paragraph 6)

   ○ "A physicist and his team then joined the discussion." (paragraph 6)
   ○ "The physicist and his team insisted that the time was actually 5:51 p.m." (paragraph 6)

MEANINGFUL INTERACTIONS CA-CCSS: ELD.PI.9-10.7.Ex

How well does the writer use language to create a sense of mystery about the identities of the nurse and the soldier in the photograph? Focus your discussion on paragraphs 4 and 5. Review the text that is boldfaced, and look for other examples of language that creates this sense of mystery. You can use the speaking frames below to help express your ideas in the discussion. Remember to follow turn-taking rules during the discussion. Then, use the self-assessment rubric to evaluate your participation in the discussion.

4   In the confusion and celebration, Eisenstaedt never got the names and addresses of the couple he photographed. Two weeks later, the photo appeared on the cover of *Life* magazine. It became the most famous kiss in American history. The main idea was to express both love and joy. The photo has become part of American culture to this day. It appears on everything from coffee mugs to calendars. People wanted to know the identity of the couple, so **the search began.** In 1979, Eisenstaedt **believed he had found the nurse,** but **the sailor's identity was unknown.** But had he actually found the nurse?

5   The **mystery** continued over the years. The question was always the same: **who were these two individuals? Their faces were almost totally hidden** in the photo. **Many people have claimed to be the couple.** Different accounts have commonly appeared in articles and books. Couples, observers, and even a forensic artist confirmed those accounts. Then *The Kissing Sailor*, a book published in 2012, identified the two, who were then in their nineties. The young sailor had impulsively grabbed a dental assistant and kissed her. The time, according to them, was about two o'clock.

- I think the word/phrase/sentence/question . . . effectively creates a sense of mystery because . . .

- The word/phrase/sentence/question . . . suggests . . .

- The word/phrase/sentence/question . . . helps to explain . . .

 SELF-ASSESSMENT RUBRIC CA-CCSS: ELD.PI.9-10.1.Ex

	4 I did this well.	3 I did this pretty well.	2 I did this a little bit.	1 I did not do this.
I expressed my ideas clearly.				
I supported my ideas using evidence from the text.				
I explained how well I thought the writer used language to create a sense of mystery about the identities of the two people in the photograph.				
I took turns sharing my ideas with the group.				

REREAD

Reread paragraphs 4–7 of "The Kiss." After you reread, complete the Using Language and Meaningful Interactions activities.

USING LANGUAGE   CA-CCSS: ELD.PI.9-10.12.b.Ex

Choose the correct word to complete each sentence.

1. The team was _____.
    ○ victorious   ○ victoriously   ○ victory

2. This is a _____ process.
    ○ method   ○ methodically   ○ methodical

3. We had a fun _____.
    ○ celebrate   ○ celebration   ○ celebratory

4. We are _____.
    ○ cheerful   ○ cheerfully   ○ cheer

5. We talked _____.
    ○ cheerful   ○ cheer   ○ cheerfully

MEANINGFUL INTERACTIONS   CA-CCSS: ELD.PI.9-10.6.a.Ex

Based on what you have read in "The Kiss," what is one of the key ideas of the article? Why are famous photographs so important? Work with partners in small groups to practice sharing and discussing your opinions, using the speaking frames. Then, use the self-assessment rubric to evaluate your participation in the discussion.

- One of the key ideas of the article is . . .

- Famous photographs are important because . . .

- I think you said that . . .

- I agree / don't agree that . . .

SELF-ASSESSMENT RUBRIC   CA-CCSS: ELD.PI.9-10.6.a.Ex

	4 I did this well.	3 I did this pretty well.	2 I did this a little bit.	1 I did not do this.
I explained a key idea clearly.				
I supported my ideas using evidence from the text.				
I expressed ideas about famous photographs in general.				
I listened to others' ideas respectfully.				

Please note that excerpts and passages in the StudySync® library and this workbook are intended as touchstones to generate interest in an author's work. The excerpts and passages do not substitute for the reading of entire texts, and StudySync® strongly recommends that students seek out and purchase the whole literary or informational work in order to experience it as the author intended. Links to online resellers are available in our digital library. In addition, complete works may be ordered through an authorized reseller by filling out and returning to StudySync® the order form enclosed in this workbook.

Reading & Writing Companion   **93**

REREAD

Reread paragraphs 4–7 of "The Kiss." After you reread, complete the Using Language and Meaningful Interactions activities.

USING LANGUAGE CA-CCSS: ELD.PII.9-10.3.Ex

Sort the sentences by their verb tense. Write the letter for each in the correct columns of the chart.

Sentence Options	
A	He **captured** a moment when a sailor and a nurse share a kiss.
B	He **captures** a moment when a sailor and a nurse share a kiss.
C	The photograph **continued** to be a cultural icon.
D	The photograph **continues** to be a cultural icon.
E	He **was capturing** a moment when a sailor and a nurse share a kiss.
F	People **wonder** about the couple in the photograph.
G	People **were wondering** about the couple in the photograph.
H	The photograph is **continuing** to be a cultural icon.
I	People **are wondering** about the couple in the photograph.

Verb	Present	Present Progressive	Past	Past Progressive
to capture		He **is capturing** a moment when a sailor and a nurse share a kiss.		
to wonder			People **wondered** about the couple in the photograph.	
to continue				The photograph **was continuing** to be a cultural icon.

MEANINGFUL INTERACTIONS   CA-CCSS: ELD.PI.9-10.1.Ex

Think about the privacy of the man and woman in the famous photograph discussed in the article "The Kiss." How do you think they might have felt about having their images made public without their permission for all these years? Provide some additional information on this topic, and try to make your comments as clear and accurate as possible.

- I think the people in the photograph might have felt . . . because . . .

- Some additional information I can add to this topic is . . .

Please note that excerpts and passages in the StudySync® library and this workbook are intended as touchstones to generate interest in an author's work. The excerpts and passages do not substitute for the reading of entire texts, and StudySync® strongly recommends that students seek out and purchase the whole literary or informational work in order to experience it as the author intended. Links to online resellers are available in our digital library. In addition, complete works may be ordered through an authorized reseller by filling out and returning to StudySync® the order form enclosed in this workbook.

Reading & Writing
Companion

95

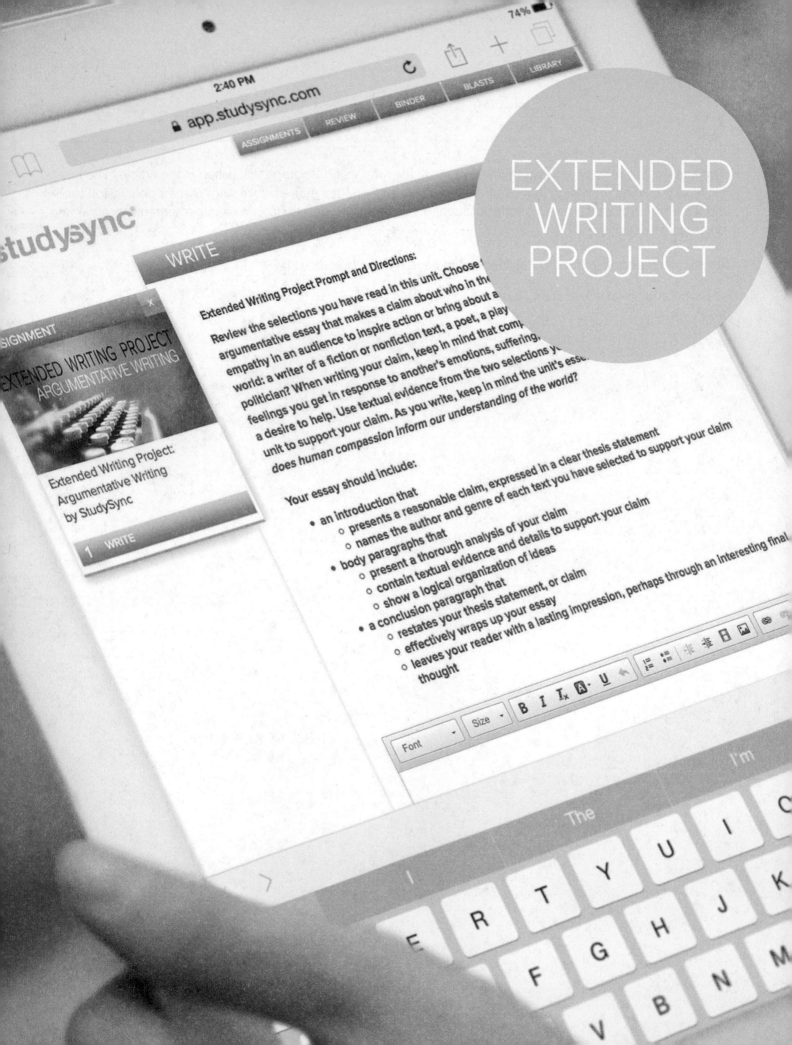

ARGUMENTATIVE WRITING

WRITING PROMPT

Review the selections you have read in this unit. Choose two selections to write an argumentative essay that makes a claim about who in the unit best evokes compassion or empathy in an audience to inspire action or bring about a deeper understanding of the world: a writer of a fiction or nonfiction text, a poet, a playwright, a photographer, or a politician? When writing your claim, keep in mind that compassion and empathy refer to the feelings you get in response to another's emotions, suffering, or misfortune combined with a desire to help. Use textual evidence from the two selections you have chosen from the unit to support your claim. As you write, keep in mind the unit's essential question: *How does human compassion inform our understanding of the world?*

Your essay should include:
- An introduction that
  › presents a reasonable claim, expressed in a clear thesis statement
  › names the author and genre of each text you have selected to support your claim

- Body paragraphs that
  › present a thorough analysis of your claim
  › contain textual evidence and details to support your claim
  › show a logical organization of ideas

- A conclusion paragraph that
  › restates your thesis statement, or claim
  › effectively wraps up your essay
  › leaves your reader with a lasting impression, perhaps through an interesting final thought

Argumentative writing is a type of nonfiction writing in which a writer establishes a strong position about a topic and develops it with paragraphs that support that position with evidence. The purpose of argumentative writing is to persuade an audience to agree that the writer's claim is sound and true. Argumentative writing can appear in many forms, including essays, speeches, debates, and letters to the editor of a newspaper.

The most important part of a strong argumentative essay is the **claim.** A claim is a writer's central argument or thesis. It communicates the main focus of the writing in clear language and allows readers to understand exactly what a writer is arguing. The claim should appear in the introductory paragraph, to help readers understand what will come next.

An argumentative essay should stay focused on the main claim and present information in a logical order that is easy for a reader to follow. Transition words help connect ideas and build the argument point by point. Effective argumentative writing includes strong evidence that supports the writer's reasoning and demonstrates if the claim is valid. It also adopts a formal tone that is appropriate to the purpose, audience, and style of this type of writing. A strong argumentative conclusion restates the writer's claim, effectively wraps up the argument, and leaves readers with a lasting impression, perhaps through an interesting final thought. The features of argumentative writing include:

- an introduction with a clear thesis statement
- clear and logical organizational structure
- supporting details, including valid reasoning and relevant textual evidence
- effective transitions to show the connection between ideas
- a formal style of writing and an objective tone
- a conclusion that restates the claim

As you continue with this extended writing project, you will receive more instructions and practice to help you craft a strong argumentative essay that includes all of these features of argumentative writing.

 STUDENT MODEL

You will learn skills of the writer's craft as you follow the writing process steps of Prewrite, Plan, Draft, and Revise, before the final step of Edit, Proofread, and Publish. Before you begin to write your own argumentative essay, start by reading this essay that one student wrote in response to the writing prompt. As you read this Student Model, highlight and annotate the features of argumentative writing that the student included in her essay.

Words to Change the World

One of the key messages an author, a poet, a playwright, an artist, a photographer, or a politician can convey to an audience is the need for human compassion or empathy to inspire action or change and to bring about a deeper understanding of humanity and the world. Precise word choice and sensory details are an author's keys to unlocking a reader's deepest emotions, but startling illustrations, paintings, or photographs can also move people. Through a news article or broadcast, words can raise public awareness of social problems, but so can photographs, for example. Which are more effective, words or pictures? The excerpt from the informational text *Endangered Dreams: The Great Depression in California*, by California historian Kevin Starr, and the article "The Harvest Gypsies," by the famous American author John Steinbeck, both inform readers about the hardships faced by migrant workers during the Great Depression. In fact, the photographs of artists like Dorothea Lange, as explained in Starr's article, allow viewers to visualize the hard lives of migrant workers in California in the 1930s. While the photographs of Dorothea Lange and artists like her provide important insights into the terrible living conditions of the migrant workers, it is the deeper human stories provided by writers such as John Steinbeck that are more effective in bringing about social change.

In *Endangered Dreams: The Great Depression in California*, Kevin Starr shows the world that photographer Dorothea Lange captured information which the photographs themselves could not contain, providing readers with insights into the subjects of Lange's pictures. Sensory details such as "a cold wet miserable day" give context for the moment when she debates the importance of turning her car around to visit the pea pickers' camp (Starr). Her "instinctive" decision to turn around leads her back to the camp, where she encounters the subject of a photograph that will eventually help change the fate of many starving migrant workers in California during the Great Depression. Starr describes the mother Lange meets as "hungry and desperate." He explains Lange's own empathy for the woman by revealing Lange's thoughts that she "seemed to know that my pictures might help her, and so she helped me. There was a sort of equality about it." While the picture went on to become known around the world, Lange's comments are absent from the image.

Starr points out that people often want words to accompany an image. "Some critics have made much of the fact that Lange did not learn the woman's name," and Starr would seem to support that criticism when he adds that she and her children were "stranded in a roadside canvas lean-to." However, Starr defends

Lange: "Such a criticism," he explains, "ignores the fact that as soon as Lange returned to San Francisco, and developed these Nipomo negatives," she told the editor at the San Francisco *News* "that thousands of pea pickers in Nipomo were starving because of the frozen harvest." Starr shows the energy of the moment, as Lange "rushed" her film to the newspaper. It was the editor, George West, who "got the story out," using two of Lange's photographs to explain what happened. The result of getting the word out was "twenty thousand pounds of food to feed the starving pea pickers" (Starr). A combination of photographs and news copy alerted the federal government, and action was taken. Words as well as photographs, Starr shows, changed America in those times of human need.

In addition to images, then, powerful words are needed to gain a public's interest in important issues. With the powerful words of his article "The Harvest Gypsies," Steinbeck presents a vivid account of the plight of families migrating through California during The Great Depression. His organization of the precise details he reveals about two particular families leads readers to a deeper understanding of the difficulties many families faced during this time. For example, Steinbeck begins his article by introducing precise words to describe a family's home: the "rot" in the "tattered" canvas held in place with "rusty" wire; the "filth" of the tent and the flies that fill the tent with their "buzzing"; the "foul clothes of the children" and "the baby, who has not been bathed nor cleaned for several days." The emphasis on the time passing in the camp, "for several days," is something a photograph could not show. When Steinbeck reveals that a four-year-old boy who was sick for weeks from lack of nourishment has died, his words capture a problem that developed over time. Steinbeck uses words to gain compassion for the parents, who now live in "paralyzed dullness." Steinbeck's repetition of "dullness" throughout the excerpt creates a continuous feeling that a single photograph, which only captures a specific moment in time, cannot communicate or express.

In his article, there are particular words Steinbeck does *not* include: He does not name any of the people he describes. While people criticized Lange for not learning the names of her subjects, Steinbeck deliberately omits the names. The decision to use only generic terms, such as "the father," "the mother," or "the child," helps readers see that these things could happen to anyone. Select details tell us that this family was once much better off—"the father of this family once had a little grocery store and his family lived in back of it so that even the children could wait on the counter"—but that the drought has caused their current extreme poverty and loss (Steinbeck). As readers, we are reminded that any of us could fall on

Copyright © BookheadEd Learning, LLC

tough times that change our lives drastically, and we are compelled to feel greater empathy for this family. Also, Steinbeck describes the family's current state as "the middle class of the squatters' camp," revealing that other families in the camp are even worse off. The writer's many details about these circumstances could not be captured in a photograph. When Steinbeck introduces us to the three-year-old son, the details he also offers could be shown in a photo: "The three year old child has a gunny sack tied about his middle for clothing. He has the swollen belly caused by malnutrition." However, providing details of agonies over time, such as being too weak to "try to get at the mucous in the eye-corners" and allowing flies to "crawl up his nose," are unique to the writer's craft.

Certainly, a powerful image crafted by a photographer, such as Dorothea Lange's *Migrant Mother*, draws a viewer in and makes it hard to look away. However, as the news story that accompanied her photos indicates, images alone are not enough to bring about social change. In addition, writers like John Steinbeck can do things that a photographer cannot, such as provide context or offer commentary on a situation he is writing about. Steinbeck says of one migrant, "He will not look directly at you for that requires will and will needs strength." The writer interprets a moment for a reader, based on evidence he himself has provided. Together, the craft of the photographer and the craft of the writer can influence how citizens respond to the needs of society, but it is words that change the world.

 ## THINK QUESTIONS

1. What is the author's claim in the Student Model? What explanation in the introduction does the author of the essay offer to support this claim?

2. How does the student author support her claim? Is her reasoning sound and her evidence sufficient? Are there any false statements? Include examples from the Student Model in your answer to explain whether or not the author has supported her claim in this essay.

3. Has the student author presented information in a logical organization that shows how her claim and evidence are related? Explain how the author has organized her essay and determine whether or not the organization is logical.

4. Think about the writing prompt. Which selections, Blasts, or other resources would you like to use to create your own argumentative essay? What are some ideas that you may want to develop in your essay?

5. Based on what you have read, listened to, or researched, how would you answer the unit's Essential Question, *How does human compassion inform our understanding of the world?* What are some selections you might explore in your essay to answer this question, and what might your focus be?

Please note that excerpts and passages in the StudySync® library and this workbook are intended as touchstones to generate interest in an author's work. The excerpts and passages do not substitute for the reading of entire texts, and StudySync® strongly recommends that students seek out and purchase the whole literary or informational work in order to experience it as the author intended. Links to online resellers are available in our digital library. In addition, complete works may be ordered through an authorized reseller by filling out and returning to StudySync® the order form enclosed in this workbook.

Reading & Writing Companion   **101**

PREWRITE

CA-CCSS: CA.RI.9-10.1, CA.RI.9-10.2, CA.W.9-10.1a, CA.W.9-10.5, CA.W.9-10.6, CA.W.9-10.9b

WRITING PROMPT

Review the selections you have read in this unit. Choose two selections to write an argumentative essay that makes a claim about who in the unit best evokes compassion or empathy in an audience to inspire action or bring about a deeper understanding of the world: a writer of a fiction or nonfiction text, a poet, a playwright, a photographer, or a politician? When writing your claim, keep in mind that compassion and empathy refer to the feelings you get in response to another's emotions, suffering, or misfortune combined with a desire to help. Use textual evidence from the two selections you have chosen from the unit to support your claim. As you write, keep in mind the unit's essential question: *How does human compassion inform our understanding of the world?*

Your essay should include:
- An introduction that
  › presents a reasonable claim, expressed in a clear thesis statement
  › names the author and genre of each text you have selected to support your claim

- Body paragraphs that
  › present a thorough analysis of your claim
  › contain textual evidence and details to support your claim
  › show a logical organization of ideas

- A conclusion paragraph that
  › restates your thesis statement, or claim
  › effectively wraps up your essay
  › leaves your reader with a lasting impression, perhaps through an interesting final thought

In addition to studying techniques authors use to build an argument, you have been reading and exploring texts that examine how writers, poets, playwrights, photographers, and politicians evoke compassion or empathy in an audience. In the extended writing project, you will use argumentative writing techniques to compose your own argumentative essay that relates to the unit theme of empathy and to the unit's Essential Question: *How does human compassion inform our understanding of the world?*

As you begin to brainstorm for your essay, think back to the selections you have read in this unit. How do these selections show how writers, photographers, or politicians evoke compassion in an audience? How do they get an audience to identify with and understand what others might be thinking or feeling? What claim can you make based on these selections? What reasons can you think of to support your claim? How will audience and purpose affect the way you develop your ideas? What specific evidence can you draw from the unit texts to support your claim?

Then complete a prewriting road map such as this one, completed by the author of the Student Model:

My Claim: A writer's words evoke stronger empathy than a photographer's pictures do.

Selections I Will Cite to Support My Claim:
Endangered Dreams: The Great Depression in California by Kevin Starr
"The Harvest Gypsies" by John Steinbeck

Reasons and Evidence from *Endangered Dreams* That Support My Claim:

- Reason: Starr's description of Lange's trip to the pea pickers' camp contains details that evoke compassion and empathy that are not present in the photograph.
- Evidence: "a cold wet miserable day" (sensory detail), "the hungry and desperate mother," that she "seemed to know that my pictures might help her, and so she helped me. There was a sort of equality about it" (Lange's own commentary, quoted by Starr)

Reasons and Evidence from "The Harvest Gypsies" That Support My Claim:

- Reason: Steinbeck's words provide readers with a deeper understanding of the difficulties faced by families during The Great Depression.
- Evidence: "buzzing" flies and "foul" children's clothes (sensory details), repetition of "dullness" and mention of the baby "who has not been bathed nor cleaned for several days" (illustrates the length of time in which the families suffered, which can't be captured by a photograph)

- <u>Reason</u>: Steinbeck's word choices remind readers that any of us could face these difficulties, creating greater reader empathy.
- <u>Evidence</u>: Use of "the father," "the mother," "the child" rather than names creates ambiguity or the feeling of nameless people who do not matter.
- <u>Reason</u>: Words and photographs can work in harmony to help us to empathize, but words have a greater impact when inspiring action or creating a deeper understanding of humanity and the world.
- <u>Evidence</u>: Lange "rushed" her photographs to the newspaper, and the editor "got the story out," prompting the government to take action to feed the starving migrant workers.

Considerations for Audience and Purpose: I should use strong, persuasive language, an objective tone, and a formal style to help persuade my audience.

SKILL:
THESIS
STATEMENT

⭐ DEFINE

The **thesis statement** is the most important sentence in an argumentative essay because it introduces what the writer is going to explore and attempt to prove in the essay or analysis. The thesis statement expresses the writer's **central or main idea** about that topic, or the **claim** the writer will develop in the body of the essay. In this way, the thesis statement of an essay acts as a road map, giving readers a view of what they will encounter throughout the essay. The thesis statement appears in the essay's introductory paragraph and is often the introduction's last sentence. The body paragraphs of the essay all support the thesis statement with specific ideas, as well as evidence to support the ideas. The thesis statement should reappear in some form in the essay's concluding paragraph.

IDENTIFICATION AND APPLICATION

A thesis statement
- makes a clear statement about the central idea of the essay.
- lets the reader know what to expect in the body of the essay.
- responds fully and completely to an essay prompt.
- is presented in the introduction paragraph and restated in the conclusion.
- is a work-in-progress and should be revised and improved, as needed, during the early stages of the writing process.

MODEL

The following is the introductory paragraph from the Student Model essay "Words to Change the World":

> *One of the key messages an author, a poet, a playwright, an artist, a*
> *photographer, or a politician can convey to an audience is the need for*

Please note that excerpts and passages in the StudySync® library and this workbook are intended as touchstones to generate interest in an author's work. The excerpts and passages do not substitute for the reading of entire texts, and StudySync® strongly recommends that students seek out and purchase the whole literary or informational work in order to experience it as the author intended. Links to online resellers are available in our digital library. In addition, complete works may be ordered through an authorized reseller by filling out and returning to StudySync® the order form enclosed in this workbook.

Reading & Writing
Companion

105

human compassion or empathy to inspire action or change while bringing about a greater understanding of the world. Precise word choice and sensory details are an author's keys to unlocking a reader's deepest emotions, but startling illustrations, paintings, or photographs can also move people. Through a news article or broadcast, words can raise public awareness of social problems, but so can photographs, for example. Which are more effective, words or pictures? The excerpt from the informational text *Endangered Dreams: The Great Depression in California,* by California historian Kevin Starr, and the article "The Harvest Gypsies," by the famous American author John Steinbeck, both inform readers about the hardships faced by migrant workers during the Great Depression. In fact, the photographs of artists like Dorothea Lange, as explained in Starr's article, allow viewers to visualize the hard lives of migrant workers in California in the 1930s. **While the photographs of Dorothea Lange and artists like her provide important insights into the terrible living conditions of the migrant workers, it is the deeper human stories provided by writers such as John Steinbeck that are more effective in bringing about social change.**

Notice the thesis statement, shown above in bold. This student's thesis statement responds to the prompt, identifying the works she will analyze in the essay and the point she will be making about the selections. It also specifically states the writer's specific central or main idea about the topic: in this writer's view, words are more effective than images in bringing about social change. This position or main claim, which appears at the end of the essay's first paragraph, sets up the rest of the essay on this topic.

 PRACTICE

Using a pen and paper, draft a complete, effective thesis statement that expresses your central idea or claim in a clear and engaging way. Be sure that your thesis statement addresses the prompt. When you are done writing, switch papers with a partner to evaluate each other's work. How clearly did your partner state the main point? Does the thesis statement answer the question or topic posed in the prompt? Does the thesis statement clearly state the focus of the rest of the essay? Offer suggestions, and remember that they are most helpful when they are informative and constructive.

SKILL:
ORGANIZE
ARGUMENTATIVE
WRITING

 ## DEFINE

The purpose of argumentative writing is to make a claim or take a position on a topic, and then to identify, evaluate, and present relevant evidence that supports the position. To do this effectively, writers need to organize and present their claims, topics, ideas, facts, details, and other information in a logical way that makes it easy for readers to follow and understand.

A strong argumentative essay contains an introductory paragraph, several body paragraphs, and a concluding paragraph. The **introductory paragraph** presents the topic and the writer's position or central claim in a **thesis statement**. The following **body paragraphs** will then support this claim with logical and valid reasoning and relevant evidence from reliable sources. Part of making a convincing argument in the body paragraphs involves distinguishing the claims from **opposing claims,** or **counterclaims**—those that are contrary to the author's position or point of view. A strong argumentative essay will explain why those counterclaims are not correct, using evidence that supports the writer's claim.

Authors organize the claims, reasons, supporting evidence, and counterclaims into an effective argument within an organizational structure that suits the topic. An argument that presents details or events in the order they occurred is using **sequential** or chronological structure. This is very effective, for example, when making a historical argument. Other structures include **compare and contrast** structure—which is useful in analyzing the similarities and differences between two authors' treatments of a topic—**problem and solution** and **cause-and-effect.**

 ## IDENTIFICATION AND APPLICATION

- The author of an argumentative essay takes a position on the topic and clearly states a claim, usually in a thesis statement in the first paragraph.

- Body paragraphs support the claim with text evidence and logical reasoning. Text evidence is factual information from the text that supports the author's claim. Some evidence is strong because it can be verified in other sources as true. Strong textual evidence may be in the form of numbers or statistics, quotes from experts, names or dates, other facts, or references to other credible sources.

- Writers select an organizational structure based on what makes sense for their topic. To choose a structure, they might ask the following questions:
  - › What is the claim or thesis that I am making about the topic?
  - › Am I comparing and contrasting different viewpoints held by different authors about the same topic, issue, or conflict?
  - › Would it make sense to relay events related to the topic in the order they occurred?
  - › What is the problem and what solutions do the authors propose?
  - › Do any natural cause and effect relationships emerge in my analysis of the topic?

- Writers often use word choice to create connections between details and hint at the organizational structure being used:
  - › Sequential order: *first, next, then, finally, last, initially, ultimately*
  - › Cause and effect: *because, accordingly, as a result, in effect, so*
  - › Compare and contrast: *like, unlike, also, both, similarly, although, while, but, however*
  - › A restatement of the claim is usually found in the concluding paragraph.

MODEL

"Words to Change the World" is an example of an argumentative essay written by a student. The writer knows from the prompt that she will be comparing the ways in which two creative people attempt to bring out compassion in their audiences. Because of this, it makes sense for her to organize her essay in a compare and contrast structure. After choosing her sources, the excerpt from Endangered Dreams by Kevin Starr and the article "Harvest Gypsies," by John Steinbeck, the writer considers the similarities and differences between the ways in which these sources generate empathy and compassion. She then uses this information to decide that, in her opinion, Steinbeck's words are a more effective way of creating empathy than Lange's images alone. She will state this position in the final sentence of her first paragraph:

In fact, **the photographs of artists like Dorothea Lange,** as explained in Starr's article, **allow viewers to visualize the hardship** faced by the migrant workers. While the photographs of Dorothea Lange and artists like her provide important insights into the terrible living conditions of the migrant workers, **it is the deeper human stories provided by writers such as John Steinbeck that are more effective in bringing about social change.**

This is her thesis statement, the most important claim that she will make in her essay. This claim sets up what will follow in the body of the text. This paragraph also identifies one counterclaim to the writer's thesis: powerful images exist and "provide important insights," and Lange's photographs "allow viewers to visualize the hardship" in a way that words do not.

In the second paragraph of her essay "Words to Change the World," the writer references *Endangered Dreams* to begin to support her argument.

In *Endangered Dreams: The Great Depression in California,* Kevin Starr shows the world that **photographer Dorothea Lange captured information which the photographs themselves cannot contain,** providing readers with insights into the subjects of Lange's pictures. **Sensory details such as "cold wet miserable day"** give context for the moment when she debates the importance of turning her car around to visit the pea pickers' camp (Starr). Her "instinctive" decision to turn around leads her back to the camp, where she encounters the subject of a photograph that will eventually help change the fate of many starving migrant workers in California during the Great Depression. Starr describes the mother Lange meets as "hungry and desperate." He explains Lange's own empathy for the woman by revealing Lange's thoughts that she "'seemed to know that my pictures might help her, and so she helped me. There was a sort of equality about it.'" While the picture went on to become known around the world, Lange's comments are absent from the image.

In this paragraph, the writer argues against the counterclaim that pictures provide something that words cannot, by presenting evidence from Starr's text, which mentions "information which the pictures themselves cannot contain." She includes details from Starr's text to show how the background information he provides serves to enhance an audience's appreciation of Lange's work. For example, familiarity with Lange's quotes can heighten the experience of viewing the photograph *Migrant Mother*. By the end of the third paragraph, she also points out that Starr's own evidence shows how a combination of photographs and news copy was needed to spur government action to help the migrants.

In the next paragraphs, the writer moves on to a discussion of Steinbeck's article "The Harvest Gypsies." This part of the essay is using mostly a compare and contrast structure, signaled by words such as "while" and references to Lange:

> In his article, there are particular words Steinbeck does *not* include: Steinbeck does not name any of the people he describes. **While people criticized Lange** for not learning the names of her subjects, **Steinbeck deliberately omits** the names. The decision to use only generic terms, such as "the father," "the mother," or "the child," helps readers see that these things could happen to anyone.

This structure allows the writer to point out critical differences in the approaches used by Steinbeck and Lange, as well as the difference in their effect on an audience.

 ## PRACTICE

Go back to the thesis statement you crafted for your argumentative essay. Consider your topic and thesis, and decide whether you will use sequential order, compare and contrast, cause-effect, or problem-solution structure to organize your paper. Draft a rough outline in which you present your thesis statement, list some of the evidence you may want to use to support the claim, and indicate at least one counterclaim. Your outline should reflect the structure you have chosen. Exchange papers with a partner and offer each other feedback. Is it clear what is being proved or disproved? Does the structure fit the topic and the thesis?

SKILL:
SUPPORTING
DETAILS

 DEFINE

Argumentative essays intend to convince readers of a writer's position or point of view on a subject. To build an argument, writers introduce **claims,** or arguments, and then support those claims with logical and valid reasoning and relevant evidence from reliable sources. Writers may also introduce **counterclaims** – claims that are contrary to the writer's point of view – and use evidence to refute, or disprove, them. Before beginning an argumentative essay, writers must search for relevant **supporting details** to support their claims. Relevant information includes facts, statistics, definitions, textual evidence, examples, or quotations that are directly related to the writer's thesis statement, or main idea.

Writers must evaluate source information to determine its reliability before using it to support a claim. A reliable source is one that is accurate, current, and comes from a credible, or believable, place. Information that comes from a reliable source and is directly related to the writer's main idea provides strong support for a claim. Personal opinions, emotional appeals, and information that may be biased provide weaker support for a claim. An argument should not rely on these kinds of support.

 IDENTIFICATION AND APPLICATION

- Supporting evidence helps writers develop and strengthen claims in an argumentative essay.
- All supporting details in an argumentative essay should directly relate to the essay's main claim, or thesis statement.
- Writers often introduce and refute counterclaims to support their own claims.
- A writer's own reasoning can provide support for a claim when it is valid and relevant.

- When planning an argumentative essay, writers should choose details that are appropriate to a particular audience.

- Text evidence is factual information from the text that supports the author's claim. Some evidence is strong because it can be verified in other sources as true. Strong text evidence may be in the form of:
  › numbers or statistics
  › quotes from experts
  › names or dates
  › other facts
  › references to other credible sources

- Weaker text evidence cannot always be proven to be true. It may be in the form of:
  › opinions
  › personal beliefs
  › emotional appeals
  › biased, or one-sided, statements

 ## MODEL

In the Student Model "Words to Change the World," the writer presents her thesis statement in the first paragraph:

> The excerpt from the informational text *Endangered Dreams: The Great Depression in California,* by California historian Kevin Starr, and the article "The Harvest Gypsies," by the famous American author John Steinbeck, both inform readers about the hardships faced by migrant workers during the Great Depression. In fact, the photographs of artists like Dorothea Lange, as explained in Starr's article, allow viewers to visualize the the hard lives of migrant workers in California in the 1930s. **While the photographs of Dorothea Lange and artists like her provide important insights into the terrible living conditions of the migrant workers, it is the deeper human stories provided by writers such as John Steinbeck that are more effective in bringing about social change.**

This statement tells readers the writer's point of view on the subject, and shows what to expect in the body paragraphs that will follow. So, what kinds of supporting details could a writer use to argue for this claim? Relevant details might include details about the effects of writers such as Steinbeck on social policies, or details that show the limits of photography in bringing change. These are the kinds of details a reader will expect to see in the rest of this argumentative essay, beginning with the first body paragraph, paragraph 2:

> In *Endangered Dreams: The Great Depression in California*, Kevin Starr shows the world that **photographer Dorothea Lange captured information which the photographs themselves could not contain,** providing readers with insights into the subjects of Lange's pictures. **Sensory details such as "cold wet miserable day"** give context for the moment when she debates the importance of turning her car around to visit the pea pickers' camp (Starr). Her "instinctive" decision to turn around leads her back to the camp, where she encounters **the subject of a photograph that will eventually help change the fate of many starving migrant workers** in California during the Great Depression. Starr describes the mother Lange meets as "hungry and desperate." He explains Lange's own empathy for the woman by revealing **Lange's thoughts that she "'seemed to know that my pictures might help her, and so she helped me. There was a sort of equality about it.'" While the picture went on to become known around the world, Lange's comments are absent from the image.**

In this paragraph, the writer provides details about Lange's photograph *Migrant Mother*, and the commentary she originally included with it. Supporting details include quotations from the text, as well as from Dorothea Lange herself. She also introduces a counterclaim. A counterclaim is a statement that argues against the writer's main claim, or thesis. In an argumentative essay, writers will often address the counterclaim, and then show that they have enough evidence to disprove it. In this case, the counterclaim is that the photograph helped "change the fate of many starving migrant workers," and that while the picture became famous, "Lange's comments are absent from the image," which is contrary to the writer's thesis that words are more important than images in bringing about social change.

In the following paragraph, then, the writer will use supporting details to refute, or disprove, this counterclaim:

> However, Starr defends Lange: "Such a criticism," Starr explains, "ignores the fact that as soon as Lange returned to San Francisco, and developed these Nipomo negatives," **she told the editor at the San Francisco *News*** "that thousands of pea pickers in Nipomo were starving because of the frozen harvest." Starr shows the energy of the moment, as **Lange "rushed" her film to the newspaper. It was the editor, George West, who "got the story out,"** using two of Lange's photographs to explain what happened. **The**

result of getting the word out was "twenty thousand pounds of food to feed the starving pea pickers" (Starr). A combination of photographs and news copy alerted the federal government, and action was taken. Words as well as photographs, Starr shows, changed America in those times of human need.

In this paragraph, the writer uses more quotations from Starr's text and from Lange to show that a "combination of photographs and news copy" is what changed things for the pea pickers, not the photograph alone. Change happened because Lange "told the editor" what was happening at the camps, and it was "getting the word out" that convinced the government to take action.

Through the use of relevant supporting details, the writer has both supported her own claim and disproven a counterclaim, building a strong case that the written (or spoken) word can be more powerful than images alone in creating compassion and bringing about change..

 ## PRACTICE

Go back to your prewriting road map, reread your main claim or replace it with your revised thesis, and evaluate the strength and relevance of the reasons and evidence you included in the road map. Copy your main claim or thesis on a new sheet, and under it, write a list of the strongest, most relevant supporting details from the road map or other sources you found after creating the road map. When you have finished, exchange lists with a partner and offer each other feedback. Which supporting detail is the most persuasive? Which is the least persuasive? Which reasons seem clear, and which seem confusing?

PLAN

CA-CCSS: CA.RI.9-10.1, CA.W.9-10.1a, CA.W.9-10.1b, CA.W.9-10.4, CA.W.9-10.9b, CA.SL.9-10.1

WRITING PROMPT

Review the selections you have read in this unit. Choose two selections to write an argumentative essay that makes a claim about who in the unit best evokes compassion or empathy in an audience to inspire action or bring about a deeper understanding of the world: a writer of a fiction or nonfiction text, a poet, a playwright, a photographer, or a politician? When writing your claim, keep in mind that compassion and empathy refer to the feelings you get in response to another's emotions, suffering, or misfortune combined with a desire to help. Use textual evidence from the two selections you have chosen from the unit to support your claim. As you write, keep in mind the unit's essential question: *How does human compassion inform our understanding of the world?*

Your essay should include:
- An introduction that
  - › presents a reasonable claim, expressed in a clear thesis statement
  - › names the author and genre of each text you have selected to support your claim

- Body paragraphs that
  - › present a thorough analysis of your claim
  - › contain textual evidence and details to support your claim
  - › show a logical organization of ideas

- A conclusion paragraph that
  - › restates your thesis statement, or claim
  - › effectively wraps up your essay
  - › leaves your reader with a lasting impression, perhaps through an interesting final thought

Please note that excerpts and passages in the StudySync® library and this workbook are intended as touchstones to generate interest in an author's work. The excerpts and passages do not substitute for the reading of entire texts, and StudySync® strongly recommends that students seek out and purchase the whole literary or informational work in order to experience it as the author intended. Links to online resellers are available in our digital library. In addition, complete works may be ordered through an authorized reseller by filling out and returning to StudySync® the order form enclosed in this workbook.

Reading & Writing Companion   **115**

As you begin to plan your argumentative essay, use your prewriting road map and list of possible supporting details to assemble your sources, your claim, and the relevant evidence you will be using to support your claim. Create an outline in preparation for writing your extended argumentative essay. At the top, state the claim you will argue. List the main topics you will address. Underneath each topic, list reasons and supporting evidence from the selections you have chosen to support your claim. Check that your outline follows logical organization for an argumentative essay. If you wish to do additional research to develop your ideas, be sure to keep a record of your sources as you place the information in the outline.

The author of the Student Model, "Words to Change the World," used an outline to organize her ideas before she started writing her essay. The outline divides evidence from the two articles the student references, in the order in which these details are presented in the articles. Note that all the evidence she cites addresses the original claim. Outlines help writers to eliminate information that is not relevant to the argument.

Look at the outline example and think about how you will outline and organize the information in your argumentative essay:

Essay Outline:

Essay Claim: While photographs can provide important insights into the human condition, it is the deeper human stories provided by writers that are more effective in bringing about social change.

Logical reasoning (to support the claim): The most important part of an outline is an explanation of the reasoning behind the argument. To support an argument, writers need to present credible, provable evidence in the form of facts, examples, quotations, statistics, studies, and other documented research to back up any claims they make.

1. Claim: Photographs can provide important insights into the human condition, but writers are more effective in bringing about social change.
    a. Compare and contrast the photographs of Dorothea Lange in *Endangered Dreams: The Great Depression in California* and John Steinbeck's article "The Harvest Gypsies."
        i. Which is more effective, words or pictures?
        ii. Word choice and sensory details can unlock a reader's emotions and raise public awareness
        iii. Startling photographs can also move people

2. Textual evidence from *Endangered Dreams*
    a. Starr provides insight into the subject of Lange's photographs that the photos alone cannot provide.

        i. Lange's decision to turn around and visit the pea pickers' camp

        ii. Explanation of Lange's empathy for her subject

        iii. Relationship between Lange and her subject

    b. Effects of Lange's photograph *Migrant Mother*

        i. Lange developed the negatives as soon as she returned to San Francisco

        ii. Tells editor of the News about the plight of pea pickers in Nipomo

        iii. Editor "gets the story out" with two of Lange's photographs

        iv. The government acts and delivers food to the pea pickers' camp

        v. Powerful words needed in addition to photographs to spark action and bring about change

3. Textual evidence from "The Harvest Gypsies"

    a. Steinbeck's use of precise details reveals plight of migrant families in California during the Great Depression.

        i. "rot" in the "tattered" canvas held in place with "rusty" wire

        ii. "filth" of the tent, "buzzing" of flies

        iii. emphasis on time passing

        iv. words capture problems that develop over time; photo captures only a single moment

    b. Details that Steinbeck deliberately omits create empathy and a sense that this could be anyone's situation at any time.

        i. Steinbeck omits names; uses only generic terms such as "mother" and "father"

        ii. Points out how family fell on hard times

        iii. Certain details that happen over time can only be revealed through a writer's craft

4. Conclusion

    a. Images alone are not enough to bring about social change.

        i. A news story accompanied Lange's photos to alert people to the conditions in Nipomo

        ii. Writers offer commentary on a situation that a photographer cannot provide through a photograph

        iii. The craft of the photographer and the writer can influence society, but it is words that change the world

Please note that excerpts and passages in the StudySync® library and this workbook are intended as touchstones to generate interest in an author's work. The excerpts and passages do not substitute for the reading of entire texts, and StudySync® strongly recommends that students seek out and purchase the whole literary or informational work in order to experience it as the author intended. Links to online resellers are available in our digital library. In addition, complete works may be ordered through an authorized reseller by filling out and returning to StudySync® the order form enclosed in this workbook.

Reading & Writing Companion   **117**

SKILL:
INTRODUCTIONS

 DEFINE

The **introduction** is the opening paragraph or section of an essay or other nonfiction text. To begin an argumentative essay, writers identify the **topic,** or what the essay will be about. For an argumentative essay, the most important part of the introduction is the **thesis statement,** which contains the writer's main claim. An essay introduction should also include a **hook,** a statement or detail that grabs the reader's attention and generates reader interest in the topic.

 IDENTIFICATION AND APPLICATION

- To set up the argument and introduce the topic, authors may offer descriptions, anecdotes, and other information to prepare the reader.
- A thesis statement often appears as the last sentence of an introduction.
- A thesis statement is not based on an author's immediate, unconsidered opinion of a topic but is instead a statement based on reasons and evidence.
- The claim in the thesis statement must be proven in the body of the essay with relevant evidence and clear reasoning.
- The introduction should leave the reader with no doubt about the author's intention.
- The introduction should engage the reader and create interest that will encourage him or her to keep reading.

 MODEL

To introduce an argument, writers need to prepare readers for the subject, the claim that will be made, and the kinds of evidence the writer will be using. The student author of the argumentative essay "Words to Change the World" has opened her argument with this introductory paragraph.

One of the key messages an author, a poet, a playwright, an artist, a photographer, or a politician can convey to an audience is the need for human compassion or empathy to inspire action or change and to bring about a deeper understanding of humanity and the world. Precise word choice and sensory details are an author's keys to unlocking a reader's deepest emotions, but startling illustrations, paintings, or photographs can also move people. Through a news article or broadcast, **words can raise public awareness of social problems, but so can photographs,** for example. Which are more effective, words or pictures? The excerpt from **the informational text** Endangered Dreams: The Great Depression in California, **by California historian Kevin Starr, and the article "The Harvest Gypsies," by the famous American author John Steinbeck,** both inform readers about the hardships faced by migrant workers during the Great Depression. In fact, the photographs of artists like Dorothea Lange, as explained in Starr's article, allow viewers to visualize the hard lives of migrant workers in California in the 1930s. **While the photographs of Dorothea Lange and artists like her provide important insights into the terrible living conditions of the migrant workers, it is the deeper human stories provided by writers such as John Steinbeck that are more effective in bringing about social change.**

The opening sentence introduces one of the main ideas of the essay: Authors and artists communicate to people "the need for human compassion or empathy to inspire action or change." This signals to the reader that the rest of the essay will address the ways in which authors and artists do just that. This statement also acts as a "hook": it is the kind of statement that readers might strongly agree or disagree with, prompting them to read further. Other "hooks" in argumentative writing might include an interesting anecdote, or a fact that might be little-known or surprising.

The writer follows her introductory sentence by saying that articles and photographs "can raise public awareness of social problems." Next, she cites the two selections she will use as source material to provide textual evidence for her essay: "The excerpt from the informational text Endangered Dreams: The Great Depression by Kevin Starr and the article "The Harvest Gypsies" by John Steinbeck." All of this builds up to the writer's claim, which is contained in the thesis statement. The reference to "terrible living conditions" and "deeper human stories" in the thesis statement are another "hook" -- a hint at some interesting topics to be discussed in the essay. Leaving the thesis statement until the end of the paragraph helps readers to transition smoothly into the writer's argument, which she will build in the body paragraphs that follow.

A strong introduction draws the readers into the topic, leaving no room for doubt about what they can expect from the rest of the text.

 PRACTICE

Write an introduction for your informative essay that introduces the topic, presents the thesis statement and the sources that will be discussed in the essay, and includes a hook. When you are finished, trade introductions with a partner and offer each other feedback. How clear is the topic? How strong is the claim made in the thesis statement? How effective was the hook in drawing you into the topic? Offer each other suggestions for improvement, and remember that they are most helpful when they are constructive.

SKILL: BODY PARAGRAPHS AND TRANSITIONS

 DEFINE

Body paragraphs are the section of the essay between the introduction and conclusion paragraphs. Body paragraphs reveal a writer's **main points** and **claims**. They also present **evidence,** or information that supports the author's claims. Each body paragraph of an essay typically presents one main point or claim, to avoid confusing the reader. The purpose of each body paragraph is to support the **thesis statement,** the main claim of the essay.

Each body paragraph of an argumentative essay should contain the following structure:

Topic sentence: The topic sentence is the first sentence of a body paragraph. It should state the main point of the paragraph and support the thesis statement or main claim of the essay.

Evidence #1: A topic sentence is followed by evidence that supports the main point. Evidence can be relevant facts, statistics, definitions, quotations, examples, or other information used to support a claim.

Reasoning #1: Evidence should be followed by reasoning, or an explanation of how that evidence supports the main point of the paragraph. This explanation should also reveal how the evidence supports the overall thesis statement, or main claim of the essay.

Evidence #2: Writers can provide further support for their main points by introducing a second piece of evidence.

Reasoning #2: Again, evidence should be followed by reasoning, or an explanation of how that evidence supports the main point, and overall, the thesis statement.

Concluding sentence: The concluding sentence of a paragraph wraps up the main idea and transitions to the next paragraph.

Transitions are connecting words and phrases that clarify the relationships among ideas in a text. Transitions help writers create an organizational structure and show readers how the information in the essay is connected. Writers use many different types of transitions to connect ideas in the body paragraphs of an argumentative essay:

- **Introductory phrases and clauses**, which begin a sentence and end in a comma, help create connections between ideas. Writers might use introductory phrases and clauses such as "Until recently," "As the results showed," or "According to" to introduce evidence and explain how the evidence supports the main point.

- **Cause-and-effect transitions** present a cause-and-effect relationship between ideas. Words such as *since, because, so, therefore, thus, hence,* and *consequently* allow writers to show how one idea leads to another. These transitions help to explain how a piece of evidence supports a point when an argument needs to show that something caused a particular result.

- **Problem and solution transitions** help writers build claims. Writers use transitions such as "so that" and "in order to" to propose solutions and support the claims in an argumentative essay.

- **Illustration transitions** help writers present evidence. Transitions such as "Such as," "For example," "For instance," and "To illustrate" connect a writer's main point in the previous sentence to the evidence that will support it.

The most effective argumentative essays will achieve their purpose—to persuade a reader to agree with the author's main claim—with well-structured body paragraphs that use strong and clear transitions to connect ideas.

 IDENTIFICATION AND APPLICATION

- The body paragraphs of an argumentative essay provide the reasons, evidence, and arguments that support the claim made in the thesis statement.
- Writers typically develop one main idea or claim per body paragraph.
- Each body paragraph contains:
  › a topic sentence to present the main idea of the paragraph
  › evidence to support the topic sentence
  › reasoning to explain how the evidence supports the main idea of the paragraph and main claim of the essay
- A body paragraph may present a counterclaim that is contrary to the thesis statement. The writer then refutes the counterclaim to support the main claim of the essay.

- The concluding sentence of a body paragraph wraps up the main idea of the paragraph, connects to the claim, and transitions to the following body paragraph.

- Writers use transition words and phrases to connect and clarify the relationships among ideas in a text.

 ## MODEL

As writers craft an argument, the way they connect ideas and information—claims, logical reasoning, and evidence—will determine whether or not their readers will be convinced. The writer of the student model essay "Words to Change the World" uses a logical structure to present the information that supports her main claim.

Look at the third paragraph of the essay:

> **Starr points out that people often want words to accompany an image.** **"Some critics have made much of the fact that Lange did not learn the woman's name,"** and **Starr would seem to support that criticism** when he adds that she and her children were "stranded in a roadside canvas lean-to." **However,** Starr defends Lange: **"Such a criticism,"** Starr explains, **"ignores the fact that as soon as Lange returned to San Francisco, and developed these Nipomo negatives,"** she told the editor at the San Francisco *News* "that thousands of pea pickers in Nipomo were starving because of the frozen harvest." **Starr shows the energy of the moment,** as Lange **"rushed"** her film to the newspaper. It was the editor, George West, who **"got the story out,"** using two of Lange's photographs to explain what happened. **The result of getting the word out** was "twenty thousand pounds of food to feed the starving pea pickers" (Starr). **A combination of photographs and news copy alerted the federal government, and action was taken. Words as well as photographs, Starr shows, changed America in those times of human need.**

This body paragraph begins with a topic sentence: "Starr points out that people often want words to accompany an image." The writer of the student model then introduces evidence from the text to support this idea: a common criticism of Lange's work, as well as Starr's own words, which "would seem to support that criticism." She then uses the transition word "However" to present a different explanation of the evidence: that Starr actually defends Lange by refuting her critics.

The writer then introduces further evidence from Starr's text, to explain that Lange "rushed" to the paper with her negatives and details of the pea pickers' plight, to help her editor craft the written news story that would accompany the photographs and eventually cause the government to take action. The phrase "the result of" shows the cause-and-effect relationship between the editor's news report and the government aid given to the pea pickers. The writer's concluding sentence returns to the ideas presented in the topic sentence: "Words as well as photographs, Starr shows, changed America in those times of human need." In illustrating this point, the body paragraph also supports the essay's thesis, which is that words are more effective than images alone in creating social change.

Now read the next paragraph of the essay:

> **In addition to images, then, powerful words are needed to gain a public's interest in important issues.** With the powerful words of his article "The Harvest Gypsies," Steinbeck presents a vivid account of the plight of families migrating through California during The Great Depression. His organization of the precise details he reveals about two particular families leads readers to a deeper understanding of the difficulties many families faced during this time in America. **For example,** Steinbeck begins his article by introducing precise words to describe a family's home: the "rot" in the "tattered" canvas held in place with "rusty" wire; the "filth" of the tent and the "exposed" human feces covered in the flies that fill the tent with their "buzzing"; the "foul clothes of the children" and "the baby, who has not been bathed nor cleaned for several days." (Steinbeck 29). The emphasis on the time passing in the camp, "for several days," is something a photograph could not show. When Steinbeck reveals that a four-year-old boy who was sick for weeks from lack of nourishment has died, his words capture a problem that developed over time. Steinbeck uses words to gain compassion for the parents, who now live in "paralyzed dullness" (Steinbeck 29). **Steinbeck's repetition of "dullness" throughout the excerpt creates a continuous feeling that a single photograph, which only captures a specific moment in time, cannot communicate or express.**

The writer presents the topic sentence that will introduce the ideas of the new paragraph: "In addition to images, then, powerful words are needed to gain a public's interest in important issues." Here the writer uses the transition "In addition to images, then" to signal a connection between ideas in the third and fourth paragraphs of the essay. The transition "For example" tells readers that the writer will now introduce evidence to support the main idea of the paragraph. As in the previous paragraph, the writer then wraps up the main idea with a strong concluding statement that explains how the textual evidence supports her thesis.

 PRACTICE

Write a body paragraph for your argumentative essay that follows the suggested format. When you are finished, trade with a partner and offer each other feedback. How effective is the topic sentence at stating the main idea of the paragraph? How strong is the evidence used to support the main idea? Does the reasoning for the evidence thoroughly support the main idea? Does the paragraph contain strong transitions to connect and clarify ideas? Offer each other suggestions and remember that they are most helpful when they are constructive.

SKILL: CONCLUSIONS

 DEFINE

No argument can be considered "won" without a strong conclusion. The **conclusion** of an argumentative essay effectively brings together the points the writer makes by summarizing or restating the thesis found in the introduction. The thesis contains the claim the writer has made, while the body of the text has offered evidence to prove that claim. The conclusion gives the final statement of the argument. For this reason, conclusions should not introduce new information. A conclusion should remind readers of the main points in the argument and support the claim in the thesis statement.

 IDENTIFICATION AND APPLICATION

- Writers often use phrases and clauses that signal cause-and-effect or summary, such as *Because of these events, As the results showed,* or *As you can see from this evidence,* to help introduce summary items in a conclusion.

- The conclusion of an argumentative essay should contain a restatement of the thesis statement.

- The conclusion of an argumentative essay should convince readers that the writer has effectively proven his or her claim.

- An essay conclusion should end in a summary statement that wraps up the ideas in the concluding paragraph. It may also end with a call to action, or statement about what the writer thinks the audience should think or do in response to the argument.

- A writer may choose to leave the reader with a final thought, to create a lasting impression on the reader.

MODEL

 NOTES

The conclusion of an argumentative essay is where a writer brings everything together: reminding readers of the writer's most important points, making final statements supporting the claim, and even using persuasive language as a way of drawing the audience's attention to these final points. Most of the time, a short, argumentative essay, such as one written for a class, will have only a single concluding paragraph. However, longer texts or different formats, such as speeches, may use more than one paragraph to develop their conclusions. Read these concluding paragraphs from Robert Kennedy's "Statement on the Assassination of Martin Luther King, Jr."

> We can do well in this country. We will have difficult times. We've had difficult times in the past, but we—and we will have difficult times in the future. It is not the **end of violence; it is not the end of lawlessness; and it's not the end of disorder.**
>
> But **the vast majority of white people and the vast majority of black people in this country want to live together,** want to improve the quality of our life, and **want justice for all human beings that abide in our land.**
>
> And let's **dedicate ourselves** to what the Greeks wrote so many years ago: **to tame the savageness of man** and make gentle the life of this world. **Let us dedicate ourselves to that**, and say a prayer for our country and for our people.

To frame his conclusion, Robert Kennedy returns to the themes of polarization and division that he used to open his statement. He notes that this act of senseless violence will not in fact be "the end of violence," and will not ultimately be the "end of disorder," but that, even so, "the vast majority of white people and the vast majority of black people in this country want to live together . . .and want justice for all human beings that abide in our land." This is a response to Kennedy's earlier mention of "polarization," or separation of the races, as one possible outcome. If people want the same thing, then they are already not "polarized." In this sentence, Kennedy attempts to convince the audience one last time that the claim he made in his thesis statement—a peaceful response is possible and is what people should do—is correct.

The final paragraph asks readers to "dedicate ourselves . . . to tame the savageness of man." This call to action refers back to the opening of the second paragraph, in which Kennedy recalls that "Martin Luther King dedicated his life to love and to justice between fellow human beings." Kennedy's final thought—his call to tame savageness and create a gentle life for all, "what the Greeks wrote"—draws on the earlier part of his speech, in which he quotes a poem by the Greek poet Aeschylus. It inspires readers to re-dedicate themselves to the goals of a fallen leader, and restates the thesis statement of his speech, which said that people should respond to this event with compassion instead of violence.

Kennedy's conclusion revisits his claim, supports it further, and ties together the main points of his entire speech, while leaving his audience with a clear call to action. Moreover, it was effective: Kennedy's audience left peacefully.

 PRACTICE

Write a conclusion for your argumentative essay. When you are finished, trade with a partner and offer each other feedback. How well did the writer restate the thesis statement? How effectively did the writer restate the main points of the essay in the conclusion? Did the writer include a summary statement to wrap up the concluding paragraph? What final thought did the writer leave you with? Offer each other suggestions, and remember that they are most helpful when they are constructive.

DRAFT

CA-CCSS: CA.W.9-10.1a, CA.W.9-10.1b, CA.W.9-10.1c, CA.W.9-10.1d, CA.W.9-10.1e, CA.W.9-10.4, CA.W.9-10.5

WRITING PROMPT

Review the selections you have read in this unit. Choose two selections to write an argumentative essay that makes a claim about who in the unit best evokes compassion or empathy in an audience to inspire action or bring about a deeper understanding of the world: a writer of fiction or nonfiction, a poet, a playwright, a photographer, or a politician? When writing your claim, keep in mind that compassion and empathy refer to the feelings you get in response to another's emotions, suffering, or misfortune combined with a desire to help. Use textual evidence from the two selections you have chosen from the unit to support your claim. As you write, keep in mind the unit's essential question: *How does human compassion inform our understanding of the world?*

Your essay should include:
- An introduction that
  › presents a reasonable claim, expressed in a clear thesis statement
  › names the author and genre of each text you have selected to support your claim

- Body paragraphs that
  › present a thorough analysis of your claim
  › contain textual evidence and details to support your claim
  › show a logical organization of ideas

- A conclusion paragraph that
  › restates your thesis statement, or claim
  › effectively wraps up your essay
  › leaves your reader with a lasting impression, perhaps through an interesting final thought

You have already made progress toward writing your own argumentative essay. You have thought about the experiences of the characters or people in the texts. You have figured out how authors, photographers, or politicians have used their writing to evoke compassion or empathy in their audience to get them to act or to better understand the world. You have decided how to organize your information and to gather supporting details. Now it's time to write a draft. Use the prewriting and planning you have done—including your road map, outline, and drafted paragraphs—to draft your argumentative essay. Be sure to include an introduction with a clear thesis statement that states your claim. Identify textual evidence and include sources of information throughout your essay. Draft a concluding paragraph that restates or reinforces your thesis statement and leaves a lasting impression on your readers. Finally, work to maintain a formal but persuasive writing style. Before you submit your draft read it over carefully. You want to be sure that you have responded to all aspects of the prompt.

When drafting, ask yourself these questions:

- How can I improve my introduction, including my "hook," so that it will "grab" my audience's attention?
- What can I do to clarify my thesis statement, or claim?
- How do my main points support my thesis statement, or claim?
- Which relevant facts, details, and quotations in each body paragraph support my main points?
- Would more precise language or different details appeal more to my audience's emotions?
- How well have I used persuasive language to convince my audience that one writer, photographer, or politician in the unit is better than another at evoking compassion or empathy in an audience?
- How effective are my transitions to create a smooth flow of ideas?
- How effective is my conclusion? Does it restate and support my claim? Does it leave my audience with a lasting impression or a call to action?
- Have I responded to all aspects of the writing prompt?

NOTES

REVISE

CA-CCSS: CA.W.9-10.1, CA.W.9-10.1d, CA.W.9-10.4, CA.W.9-10.5, CA.W.9-10.9, CA.SL.9-10.1, CA.L.9-10.2a

WRITING PROMPT

Review the selections you have read in this unit. Choose two selections to write an argumentative essay that makes a claim about who in the unit best evokes compassion or empathy in an audience to inspire action or bring about a deeper understanding of the world: a writer of a fiction or nonfiction text, a poet, a playwright, a photographer, or a politician? When writing your claim, keep in mind that compassion and empathy refer to the feelings you get in response to another's emotions, suffering, or misfortune combined with a desire to help. Use textual evidence from the two selections you have chosen from the unit to support your claim. As you write, keep in mind the unit's essential question: How does human compassion inform our understanding of the world?

Your essay should include:
- An introduction that
  › presents a reasonable claim, expressed in a clear thesis statement
  › names the author and genre of each text you have selected to support your claim

- Body paragraphs that
  › present a thorough analysis of your claim
  › contain textual evidence and details to support your claim
  › show a logical organization of ideas

- A conclusion paragraph that
  › restates your thesis statement, or claim
  › effectively wraps up your essay
  › leaves your reader with a lasting impression, perhaps through an interesting final thought

NOTES

You have written a draft of your argumentative essay. You have also received input from your peers about how to improve it. Now you are going to revise your draft.

Here are some recommendations to help you revise:

- Reread your draft before beginning your revision.
- Review the suggestions made by your peers. Make any adjustments you feel are needed.
- Evaluate the strength of your introduction and revise if necessary.
- Revise your thesis statement, if needed, to state your claim more clearly.
- Review and adjust the main points and reasoning in the body paragraphs of your essay, to be sure they are well organized and support your thesis statement, or claim.
- Examine the evidence you have provided in support of your main points and determine how your evidence could be more convincing.
- Write a strong conclusion that follows from and supports the argument you presented.
- Review and revise your transitions, to be sure they show strong and logical connections between (or among) ideas.
- Focus on maintaining a formal style, which means eliminating slang and informal expressions. A formal style suits your purpose--your reason for writing your argumentative essay--and also fits your audience, which is made up of students, teachers, and other readers interested in learning more about your topic.
- Maintain an objective tone by presenting both texts and ideas fairly.
- Consult a print or an online style manual to check guidelines for formatting and for placing in-text citations and bibliographic citations on a Works Cited page.
  › For in-text citations, be sure you have applied quotation marks or italics and parentheses correctly and have included accurate page numbers, if available.
  › For bibliographic citations, be sure that every source contains all essential information and is formatted according to the style manual's guidelines.

NOTES

EDIT, PROOFREAD, AND PUBLISH

CA-CCSS: CA.RI.9-10.1, CA.W.9-10.1, CA.W.9-10.4, CA.W.9-10.5, CA.W.9-10.9b, CA.L.9-10.1a, CA.L.9-10.1b, CA.L.9-10.2a, CA.L.9-10.2c, CA.L.9-10.3a

WRITING PROMPT

Review the selections you have read in this unit. Choose two selections to write an argumentative essay that makes a claim about who in the unit best evokes compassion or empathy in an audience to inspire action or bring about a deeper understanding of the world: a writer of a fiction or nonfiction text, a poet, a playwright, a photographer, or a politician? When writing your claim, keep in mind that compassion and empathy refer to the feelings you get in response to another's emotions, suffering, or misfortune combined with a desire to help. Use textual evidence from the two selections you have chosen from the unit to support your claim. As you write, keep in mind the unit's essential question: *How does human compassion inform our understanding of the world?*

Your essay should include:

- An introduction that

  › presents a reasonable claim, expressed in a clear thesis statement

  › names the author and genre of each text you have selected to support your claim

- Body paragraphs that

  › present a thorough analysis of your claim

  › contain textual evidence and details to support your claim

  › show a logical organization of ideas

- A conclusion paragraph that

  › restates your thesis statement, or claim

  › effectively wraps up your essay

  › leaves your reader with a lasting impression, perhaps through an interesting final thought

Please note that excerpts and passages in the StudySync® library and this workbook are intended as touchstones to generate interest in an author's work. The excerpts and passages do not substitute for the reading of entire texts, and StudySync® strongly recommends that students seek out and purchase the whole literary or informational work in order to experience it as the author intended. Links to online resellers are available in our digital library. In addition, complete works may be ordered through an authorized reseller by filling out and returning to StudySync® the order form enclosed in this workbook.

Reading & Writing Companion   **133**

You have already made great progress toward completing your argumentative essay. You have figured out how writers, photographers, or politicians in the unit have evoked compassion or empathy in their audience to get them to act or take a stand, or to better understand the world. Now it's time to edit and proofread your essay to produce a final version. As you revised your essay, did you include all the valuable suggestions from your peers? Here are some other questions for you to consider:

- Does my essay follow the basic structure of an argumentative essay: introduction, body paragraphs, and conclusion?
- Does my introduction grab my audience's attention?
- Is my thesis statement (or claim) clearly stated in my introduction and restated in my conclusion?
- Is my argument persuasive? What more can I do to improve my essay's main points, reasons, textual evidence, and organization to make my argument more convincing?
- Have I accurately cited my sources within the body of my essay and in my Works Cited page?
- Have I used appropriate and smooth transitions to connect my ideas within paragraphs as well as between paragraphs?
- Is my writing style and language formal and my tone objective?
- Have I presented my audience with a conclusion that summarizes my purpose or intent and leaves them with a final thought that will create a lasting impression?
- Does my thesis (or claim) respond completely to the writing prompt?

When you are satisfied with your essay, edit and proofread it for errors. Check that you have used correct grammar, usage, capitalization, and punctuation. Also check that your formatting is correct and that you have used correct punctuation for quotations, sources, and citations. For example, have you used italics correctly? Have you correctly used stylistic conventions that conform to the guidelines in a style manual (such as the *MLA Handbook*)? Be sure to correct any misspelled words, including compound words, while you are editing and proofreading your essay.

Once you have made all your corrections, you are ready to submit and publish your work. You can distribute your writing to family and friends, hang it on a bulletin board, or post it online or on your own blog. If you publish online, create links to your sources and citations. That way, your audience can follow up on what they have learned from your essay and read more on their own.

Text Fulfillment
Through StudySync

If you are interested in specific titles, please fill out the form below and we will check availability through our partners.

ORDER DETAILS

Date:

TITLE	AUTHOR	Paperback/ Hardcover	Specific Edition *If Applicable*	Quantity

SHIPPING INFORMATION

Contact:

Title:

School/District:

Address Line 1:

Address Line 2:

Zip or Postal Code:

Phone:

Mobile:

Email:

BILLING INFORMATION   ☐ *SAME AS SHIPPING*

Contact:

Title:

School/District:

Address Line 1:

Address Line 2:

Zip or Postal Code:

Phone:

Mobile:

Email:

PAYMENT INFORMATION

☐ CREDIT CARD   Name on Card:

Card Number: Expiration Date: Security Code:

☐ PO   Purchase Order Number:

StudySync Text Fulfillment, BookheadEd Learning, LLC
610 Daniel Young Drive | Sonoma, CA 95476